Like Father, Like Sons

Like Father, Like Sons

BY
Jim Essian

LUCIDBOOKS

To my father

Thank you for leading me to the Father.

CONTENTS

PART THREE

PREFACE

THIS IS a book written specifically for the young parents of The Paradox Church. As a relatively new parent myself, I was blown away by the grace of God that has revealed to me, ever more clearly, my adoption as His son. I do not want any of our people to miss that opportunity. I want our young fathers and mothers to see the Father's love for them.

Specifically, it is written from a daddy to daddies. However, I feel a mother could, and should, read it also, and I believe she would benefit from it. The majority of the truths and principles are completely transferrable to moms.

It is evident that God has ordained our church to be a place where He sends very broken people. The amount of abuse and rape, pornography, and sexual sin that we deal with is heartbreaking. Our prayer in planting the church was that God would send us folks who are walking through those very things—and He has—but also that He would be faithful to saturate our Body with great grace, and to flex His power and do a great work in and through us. In the two years of The Paradox Church, through our Redemption Group ministry and other counseling we have done, it is apparent that there is one great deficit that is a common denominator to the majority of struggles our people are facing: Fathers.

Many of their fathers were decent men but did not know the Gospel of Jesus, and so they did not lead their families centered on the Person and Work of the Son. Some were abusive or not protective of their children. Some were not even there. The reality is that our new dads and our new moms have not experienced godly parenting. To compound that, the doctrines of "adoption" and "God as our Father" are truths we say we believe but not realities we understand and are transformed by.

This book is meant to lay that foundation. The Christian life is a life lived by the power of the Holy Spirit, through the redemptive work of the Son, and to the Father—He is a Father to the fatherless, and we are His adopted sons.

GOD IS YOUR FATHER

"Whoever has seen me has seen the Father" — Jesus

M Y FATHER was an angry kid growing up. He told me that once. It is funny how you remember seemingly random comments from your dad as you recollect your childhood. Perhaps it stayed with me because the man I knew growing up did not seem angry, but was tender (tough as well, but in the good way), loving, and present. Anger accompanied him, but it was a "being sanctified" version of it. What changed?

Early into his adult life, my dad began searching. He probably didn't know what he was searching for at the time, but he knew he needed something. Entering adulthood in the '70s as a professional baseball player afforded him an abundance of opportunities, avenues, and religions to search out; he had a sort of Solomonic exploration before him—a tour of life under the sun.

I don't know everything. Perhaps, like Solomon, hedonism didn't work out. Maybe next he tried work and success; it is difficult to get more successful than being a 24-year-old Major League baseball player. At some point, his search for God began. It initially led him to Eastern religions like Transcendental Meditation—kind of like yoga without the mat and class fee. Eventually, a teammate of his started telling him about Jesus. Wayne Gross probably had no idea the spiritual legacy he was leaving with my dad; the Oakland A's third baseman was merely being a faithful servant of our Lord Jesus. Once the Spirit opened up my parents' eyes to the reality of the grace of the Father given in the Son, the Gospel collided with their souls and they were changed.

It was upon *seeing the Father* that my father ended his search. Solomon prosed, "All is vanity and a striving after wind, there is nothing to be gained under the sun." But my father experienced Fatherhood beyond the sun—and it changed him. The father I knew reflected a vague image of a past anger, sinfulness that was in the process of being put to death by the

Spirit, and a shadow of the young man that searched out fulfillment in pleasure or self-glory. Now, changed by the Son, he imaged and reflected the Father well to me, his son.

SLO-POKES, SLURPEES, & MELLOW MUSHROOM

Every Thursday night my dad would take me and my sister to 7-11 for a Slurpee and a Slo-Poke. Do you remember Slo-Pokes? Carmel on a stick; a brilliant invention. There were two reasons why Thursday nights were such a big deal: One, we were not allowed to have sweets at home but on Thursday nights we got candy; two, *we were with our daddy.*

We would get into his 1979 silver Mercedes station wagon with the seats down in the back and look out at the car behind us, enjoying the feeling of being chauffeured by our dad to our dining place of choice. He could have given us a Slo-Poke and a Coke at home, but it was a big deal to walk into the store and have him pay at the counter. He would talk to us on the car ride and we had daddy's sole attention. Subconsciously, I was taking notes: *"Fathers want to be with their children."*

We eat a lot of Mellow Mushroom in my house. It is the best pizza ever. Literally, it would change your life. I usually take my oldest, Harper (2) with me to pick up the pizza. It is a big deal for her to go on a car ride with daddy, and it gives mama a break from at least one of the girls (we also have Hollis, 6 months). After the first few times that we went together, I noticed that Harper would say "sit" on our way out of the restaurant to go home and eat. I would say, "No, we have to go home so we can eat." I finally realized that she wanted us to sit, not because she was hungry and did not care if mama got any, but because that made it a "date daddy."

I try to take Harper on a date every week, she calls it "date daddy." Sometimes our dates are something small, like a stroller ride to the park or walking to the doughnut shop ("doughNUTS, daddy!"), or I will make it a bigger deal, like going to the museum or to Central Market to go on the slide and get something to eat. Therefore, for her, going to Mellow Mushroom looks like a date, and it is a big deal if we sit down and eat. Now, sometimes we will sit and share a slice and then go home to eat with the rest of the family. Harper doesn't care about Mellow Mushroom, it could be any pizza. She just wants to spend time with daddy. *"Children want to be with their daddies."*

ॐ ॐ

I was unprepared for the revelations the Father would open my eyes to as a father to my girls. When I rock my girls, why does the Spirit of God whisper truths about God the Father to me?

"I care for you like this."

"I have loved you infinitely more than this for infinitely more time than you can fathom."

"You give me joy like she gives you joy."

What great grace! I am amazed at the joy my girls give me. But what is hard to believe is that I might bring the Father joy. Yet, the Scriptures insist that His children do:

> "The LORD your God is in your midst,
> a mighty one who will save;
> *he will rejoice over you with gladness;*
> he will quiet you by his love;
> *he will exult over you with loud singing.*"
> (Zephaniah 3:17)

I love hearing my wife sing over our babies; what a sweet sound! Though I sound like a goat and a chicken arguing, I sing over them as well. I like to make up songs and try to rhyme—straight free-stylin' for my girls. What joy they bring! Laughter from your child is a healing balm to anything you endured that day. So, if our children bring us such joy, is it so hard to believe that we—God's adopted sons—bring the Father joy?

But this is only seeing the perspective of a father to a son; what does the *son* see when looking at the father?

SEEING THE FATHER

I can vividly recall a common scene from my childhood: My dad on his bed, propped up by a few pillows, the smell of Skoal Wintergreen (he was a baseball player, you know?), bible commentaries and dictionaries surrounding him, and a legal pad and bible on his lap as he studied Hebrews for the weekly bible study in our home. People were saved in our home. Prayer was normal. Worship was commonplace. A dad being led by *the* Dad is a special thing.

But what you see when you hear the word "father" and what I see could be like two trains passing each other going in opposite directions. They look the same, and are doing some of the same things, but what is the purpose of a train if not to get somewhere? The destinations are different. Your father may not have been the train leading you to *the* Father.

We want to get to our Heavenly Dad. We want to be like Him; we want to know Him, but we might have been put on the wrong train. How do we see the Father to get to Him if we are going the wrong way? It is not easy to see the Father, it is not so black and white. We don't just see black (our imperfect, maybe really bad father) and white (the perfect Heavenly Father). We see the Father *through* our earthly father. We are all given lenses at some point in our childhood, and we still wear them, even as we begin to father our own children. The lenses gray our understanding of the Father. Who is He? What does He think of me? Does He accept me? Is He proud of me? What does He want from me?

In Ephesians 3:14-15 Paul prays, "For this reason I bow my knees before the Father [*patēr*], from whom every family [*patria*] in heaven and on earth is named." Tony Reinke points out that in the Greek it is easy to pick up on Paul's *patēr/patria* play on words.[1] John Stott chose to translate this phrase as "the Father from whom all fatherhood is named." God's fatherhood is the archetype of human fatherhood.

What do we do, then, with the glasses we have been given? An archetype is nice, but we live in reality, and the prototype was our father, Adam—and we all know how that went. If our father was a disciplinarian type, we tend to default to thinking God is that way. Or, if our dad was distant and not very present, we may think God is "out there" and not immanent. "Perhaps He doesn't care too much about me," we think. How do we take the glasses off to see? Furthermore, even if we could see with untrammeled sight, do we even know what the Father is *for*? Or, what *fathers* are for? Moms give birth, nourish, comfort, caress, and nurture, but what do fathers do?

WHAT ARE FATHERS FOR?

Before we can know what *fathers* are for, we need to know what the *Father* is for. Douglas Wilson asks the same question:

> "For through him [Jesus] we both have access in one Spirit to the Father" (Eph. 2:18). Think of it this way. The Son is the road. The Father is the city we are driving to, and the Spirit is the car. We are going to the Father, the Son is the way we are to go, and the Spirit enables us to go ... [yet], among Christians who believe the Bible,

there are movements that emphasize a personal relationship with Jesus—the evangelicals, for example. There are movements that emphasize the Holy Spirit—the charismatic movement. *But among conservative believers, what movement emphasizes the Father?"*[2]

The reason there is not a particular movement that emphasizes the Father, as Wilson will later point out, is that we don't understand what the Father is for. Because we don't understand what the Father is for, we don't understand fully what fathers are for. So, what is God the Father for? Answer: He is for His glory, and His glory is in His Son. Don't believe me?

" . . . the light of the knowledge of the glory of God in the face of Jesus Christ." (2 Corinthians 4:6)

"And now, Father, glorify me in your own presence with the glory that I had with you before the world existed." (John 17:5)

"He [Jesus] is the radiance of the glory of God . . ." (Hebrews 1:3)

"The infinite happiness of the Father consists in His enjoyment of the Son." — Jonathan Edwards

First, and most obviously, what this means for us is that we should be all about the Son, just as the Father is, and we should be pointing our children to the glory of God in the face of Christ over and over and over—that is godly parenting in a nutshell; show your sons the Son. Secondly, if the Father is for His glory and His glory is His Son, then shouldn't we be *for* our children? Shouldn't the way we are for them be determined by how the perfect Father is for the perfect Son? Furthermore, is the perfect Father any different towards us, his *imperfect* sons? We also are the glory of God: "For a man ought not to cover his head, si*nce he is the image and glory of God . . .*" (1 Cor. 11:7).

WHAT IS THE FATHER LIKE?

The Father is *for* His glory and His glory is in the Son. This helps us to know what the purpose of fathers are so we can best image the Father. But what is the Father *like*? This determines everything: It shapes our identity, facilitates our parenting, informs everything we do, determines how we respond, and rules over our thoughts and motives. How the Father is toward us means everything! In fact, the Father's love toward us is so strong that it will change us and conform us to the perfections of His perfect Son.

"For those whom he foreknew he also *predestined to be conformed to the image* of his Son, in order that he might be the firstborn among many brothers" (Rom. 8:29). Your conformity to Christ is a divine certainty, it will happen!

We need to see the Father clearly, sans the glasses. We cannot let the lenses of our fathers distort the image of the True Father. However, at the same time, we need to see our sonship *through the lens* of the Son's work on the cross, for this is how the Father sees us. He is for His glory, His glory is in His Son, and His glory is most evidenced in the Son's saving of many sons. This is the beauty of the Gospel: In Christ our lenses are removed so we can clearly see the Father, *and*, in Christ, the Father *puts on* lenses and sees us through His perfect Son!

This means that in the Gospel we can see what the Father is like. If we can see the Father, we can image Him to our children.

So the question that this book will answer is, "What is our Father like?" If how He is toward us conforms us to the perfect image of His Son, then it will shape how we father our children. Let's take the glasses off.

REFLECTION QUESTIONS

1. What are some big memories of your dad? Why are they so important to you?

2. How was your father (passive, gentle, distant, sacrificial, abusive, rigid, not present)? In what ways do you project that image upon God the Father?

PART ONE

YOUR FATHER IS GENEROUS

"Fathers are not looking for excuses to say no.
Their default mode is not no."
— Douglas Wilson

YOUR HEAVENLY Father gives. He gives life and breath. He has given us creation at which to marvel. Food to eat. Drink to drink. Shelter. Clothes (if the lilies of the field are clothed in splendor, how much more will He clothe us?). God gives. He gives His Son (John 3:16, 18:11), He gives His Spirit (John 14:16-17), and He gives Himself (John 14:22-24). Our Father is generous:

> "Or which one of you, if his son asks him for bread, will give him a stone? Or if he asks for a fish, will give him a serpent? If you then, who

are evil, know how to give good gifts to your children, how much more will your Father who is in heaven give good things to those who ask him!" (Matthew 7:9-11)

We bear a semblance of the image of God and so give good things to our children—innately we desire to. However, because that image of our Father is distorted from sin ("you who are evil"), we only give so much. Our generosity is truncated by our selfishness and hoarding, rendering our generosity a cheaper imitation, and our children pay for it.

How can this play out? We desire to give of our time until it becomes a sacrifice; we are tired, stressed, and need some "alone time"; so, if we do capitulate to their needy demands for "daddy time," it is done begrudgingly or not at all. Vacations and the memories that they breed take a back seat to our desire for a new car, lots of golf, big toys, or whatever we want that costs money—and it "costs" our children a family vacation. Our Father is not so stingy. His default is yes, and ours should be also.

"What are fathers called to? Fathers give. Fathers protect. Fathers bestow. Fathers yearn and long for the good of their children. Fathers delight. Fathers sacrifice. Fathers are jovial and open handed. Fathers create abundance, and if lean times come, they take the leanest portion themselves and create a sense of gratitude and abundance for the rest. Fathers love birthdays and Christmas because it provides them with yet another excuse to give more to the kids. When fathers say no, as good fathers do from time to time, it is only because they are giving a more subtle gift, one that is a bit more complicated than a cookie. They must also include among their gifts things like self-control, discipline, and a work ethic, but they are giving these things, not taking something else away just for the sake of taking. Fathers are not looking for excuses to say no. Their default mode is not no."[3]

CHAPTER ONE

BE GENEROUS WITH YOUR TIME

"In the fear of the Lord one has strong confidence, and his children will have a refuge."
— Proverbs 14:26

WHEN I walk through the black front door of our cottage-style home, I am certain of what the next few moments will look like. As soon as my oldest daughter sees me (and, yes, sometimes I stall at the door or make a loud noise to get her attention), she comes running toward me, giggling and smiling, curly-hair curls bouncing, ready for daddy to scoop her up. It is a homecoming to trump all homecomings.

I have tried to set a precedent of kissing mama first, but it is impossible when your daughter sprints (waddles fast) to you in so much joy—joy of what? Daddy's presence.

There is no other explanation. I don't ever come home with candy; I bear no gifts; it hasn't been a long absence; I am just there.

THERE-NESS

I am convinced that one of a father's greatest gifts to his children is his "there-ness." Your quantifiable there-ness is your canon as a father—a measuring rod—the ruler that determines the exactness of your fathering. You may know nothing about parenting, but if you are present you have run ahead of the curve, and good stuff can happen.

Consider the times you have felt closest to your Heavenly Father, those times the Holy Spirit graciously opened up your mind and heart to the reality of the Father's presence. Perhaps it was through fervent prayer in difficult times; maybe it was through corporate worship; maybe it was through the preaching of the Word. How was it? Did you feel safe? Secure? Approved of in Christ? Affirmed by the Father of fathers?

Did God give you anything in those times? Was He blessing you with something in creation or answering a prayer? No, *He was just there.* The Father's there-ness made everything else fade out, out of focus, inconsequential. Like being unaware of the stresses of work as you stand on a shore overlooking the vastness of the glory of the ocean; or the terrifying combination of awe and fear as you stand before the Grand Canyon, all else a mere blip on a screen as an orchestra of peace floods you from all sides. It is His there-ness that we desire.

The message of the Gospel is that we get God. Reconciliation with the Father is one of the facets of the crown jewel the cross provides us. Moses wanted nothing to do with the Promised Land if God was not going to be there (Ex. 33:15-16)—God *is* the Promised Land. Heaven is not heaven without God—it is hell.

WANTING THE FATHER'S PRESENCE

Your deepest desire is the Father's presence. How else do you explain your sacrifice or the pouring out of your time, energy, and money? We bleed out for *shadows of the Father's presence,* when what we really desire is Him. Let me explain.

Your pursuit of beauty transfigures to lust with your sinful heart. But that deep desire for beauty is a godly desire—permit me to even use a feminine term—a *yearning* for true beauty. What you want is to be in the presence of true beauty and perfection. For what is beauty but the eye's search for perfection? (And what is pornography but the sinful heart's search for the perfect woman—this one's eyes, that one's hair, the other's figure.) Created beauty flows from the Creator's perfection; you ultimately desire the beauty of His presence.

Your pursuit of affirmation, fame, acceptance and all their cousins is a deep desire to be in the presence of the Father. It is a deep longing in your heart to even be allowed in the presence of your Father, to approach boldly the throne of grace, and to be received as a son of God. Isn't it? Why else do you pursue success? For your glory, that is certain, but you also do it for acknowledgment, applause, and that sense of approval—"I'm proud of you" would bring many men to tears. These pursuits terminate on the Father. As C.S. Lewis says:

> "The books or the music in which we thought the beauty was located will betray us if we trust to them; it was not in them, it only came through

them, and what came through them was longing. These things—the beauty, the memory of our own past—are good images of what we really desire; but if they are mistaken for the thing itself they turn into dumb idols, breaking the hearts of their worshippers. For they are not the thing itself; they are only the scent of a flower we have not found, the echo of a tune we have not heard, news from a country we have never yet visited."[4]

Ecclesiastes 3:11 says that God put eternity into the heart of man. We search and search; we lust and lust; we are pursuing affirmation, fame, and acceptance. We run hard after the shadows, our feet stomping loud enough to deafen the echoes of a heart that is still unfulfilled, a soul not satisfied with shadows, but only with Substance. Chasms pervade the souls of men echoing their heart's demand for the Eternal to fill it—for the Omni Present to abide. And abide He does; for that is His gift to us—Himself. The presence of all that we desire is ultimately found in Him.

So how do we image the Father to our children? We image Him with our there-ness. What security, what protection, what joy our children find in our presence! As our joy is complete when we abide in Him (John 15:1-11), so do they sense the Father's love in us—perfected more and more in their joy with every hug-filled, playful, pile-driving minute.

BASEBALL AND BOB ROSS

I attended three schools a year for a while. My dad was managing in professional baseball and decided early on that the family being together was worth the sacrifice, struggle, and difficulty of constantly having to travel and change schools, and the security of a "normal" home life.

Of course, I loved it. It was normal for me. Home was the clubhouse and the smell of pine tar, or the luggage rack on the bus where I would sleep as the team went from town to town. Home was watching my dad play cards on a cooler set in the aisle, covered with a towel to keep the cards from sliding off, holding a beer can in his lap. His there-ness far exceeded any inconvenience. How could anything else be an option?

After watching Bob Ross paint a "happy squirrel" and my sister and I trying to paint along—a kind of "paint by Ross" version of paint by numbers—I would take a quick afternoon nap and then head to the park with dad in time for batting practice. The nap was necessary because I would be at the park until about 11 o'clock at night.

I would hang out in his office, shag fly balls during batting practice, be the batboy for the game; occasionally I would see him get thrown out of a game for arguing with the umpire, or light up one of his players for some particular reason (usually disrespect of some kind, "This is a monologue, not a dialogue!").

Child psychologists would probably sniff their noses at my childhood, like dogs smelling meat, ready to pounce: "Children need stability!" Yes, they do, and the father is to be the anchor.

SECURE AS SOJOURNERS

The Father's children aren't at home either (1 Pet. 2:11). Furthermore, our well-being doesn't necessitate wealth, possessions, the best schools, or people who approve of us. What anchors us, why we are secure, why we are commanded countless times, "Do not fear!" is that the Father is with us.

See, it is easy to excuse your lack of there-ness with your desire to "give your children a better life" or "make sure they can get the best education." Those are well-meaning desires, and a father should work hard to leave a good legacy to his children. We should plan well, save well, and block for our family like a bull-headed fullback paves the way for the tailback to get up field. That approach only works, however, if you are playing the same game, and if the goal is the end zone of our children knowing the Father—for that to happen, you have to be there.

I have never met someone who hated their father because he didn't buy them a nice car; I have, however, met plenty of people with jacked up lives and relationships—with a degree from a reputable university hanging on the wall—because their dad was not ever home.

Paul Tripp tells a similar story:

> *"When I speak in churches, I often single out the men and challenge, 'Some of you are so busy in your careers that you're seldom home, and when you are, you are so physically exhausted that you have nothing to offer your children. You don't even know your own kids. I offer a radical challenge to you. Go to your boss and ask for a demotion. Take less pay. Move out of that dream house and into a smaller one. Sell your brand new car and drive an older one. Be willing to do what God has called you to do in the life of your children.'*
>
> *In a culture with two-income families, increasingly that challenge must also be made to women who also sacrifice family for career.*

I made that appeal at one home-school conference and it angered a man in the crowd, although I didn't know it at the time. Two years later he came over to me during a conference break. As he got closer, he began to weep. He said, 'Two years ago I heard you give the challenge you just gave tonight and I got angry. I thought, What right do you have to say that? But I was haunted by your words. I thought, He's speaking about me. My whole life is away from the home and I don't know my own kids. I finally went to my boss one morning and said, 'I want to talk to you about my position.' My boss said, 'Look, we've advanced you as much and as fast as we can.' And I said, 'No, no, just hear me, I want a demotion.' The boss looked startled. He asked, 'What are you talking about?' I said, 'The most important thing in my life is not this job. The most important thing is that God has given me five children. I'm His instrument in forming their souls. But right now, I don't even know my own kids.'

The boss said, 'I've never heard this kind of conversation before and I'll probably never hear it again. I'm very moved. We'll find you a position where you can work forty hours a week. You can punch in and punch out and have less responsibility. But I'm not going to be able to pay you enough.' I said, 'That's fine.'

We sold the house of our dreams, got rid of two luxury cars and bought a mini-van. It's been two years now, and not one of my kids has come to me and said 'Dad, I wish we lived in a big house,' or 'Dad, I wish we had new cars.' But over and over again they have come and said, 'Dad, we've been having so much fun with you. It's great to have you around.' Now, for the first time, I can say I know exactly where my children are. I know their hearts. I know what I need to be doing in their lives. I'm actually being a father."[5]

The Gospel is not a call to comfort. It is news that the Father wants to be with us and will sacrifice even His Son to do so. However, it is also a call to join the Father in what He is doing—saving sinners for His glory. He is not so concerned with our comfort, or our safety; He is not always concerned we are at the perfect church (His "school" for us); He is not losing sleep over how much He *could* provide us (for some, He gives great wealth, for others, just what they need to get by). He does, however, promise His presence is with us. Look at the shear tonnage of verses explicitly stating God's there-ness and the context of the promise:

> "Be strong and courageous. Do not fear or be in dread of them, for it is the LORD your God who goes with you. *He will not leave you or forsake you.*" (Deuteronomy 31:6)

> "No man shall be able to stand before you all the days of your life. Just as I was with Moses, so *I will be with you.* I will not leave you or forsake you . . . do not be frightened, and do not be dismayed, *for the LORD your God is with you wherever you go.*" (Joshua 1:5,9)

> "Behold, I am with you and will keep you wherever you go, and will bring you back to this land. *For I will not leave you* until I have done what I have promised you." (Genesis 28:15)

> "Then David said to Solomon his son, 'Be strong and courageous and do it. Do not be afraid and do not be dismayed, *for the LORD God, even my God, is with you.* He will not leave you or forsake you, until all the work for the service of the house of the LORD is finished.'" (1 Chronicles 28:20)

"Keep your life free from love of money, and be content with what you have, for he has said, '*I will never leave you nor forsake you.*'" (Hebrews 13:5)

"And Jesus came and said to them, 'All authority in heaven and on earth has been given to me. Go therefore and make disciples of all nations, baptizing them in the name of the Father and of the Son and of the Holy Spirit, teaching them to observe all that I have commanded you. And behold, *I am with you always, to the end of the age.*'" (Matthew 28:18-20)

The call is never to comfort. In fact, quite the opposite. The demands are great: Leading people into the Promised Land, building a great temple that foreshadows Christ, obeying a radical call to contentment with money, and making disciples of all nations. The anchor in these great calls of sacrifice, discomfort, and lack of security is the presence of God. We could have all the money in the world, the best education, the safest (and nicest) cars, and still drift out to sea, the weight of all that "stuff" drowning us—we need the Anchor.

QUANTITY TIME WITH OUR CHILDREN

Quality time is a myth; your children need quantity time. You are their anchor. Your there-ness makes them feel safe, loved, and cared for. Furthermore, your calling is to disciple them. This means they are to go with you as you do life. Your children are not some slice of a pie that can be compartmentalized from the other pieces.

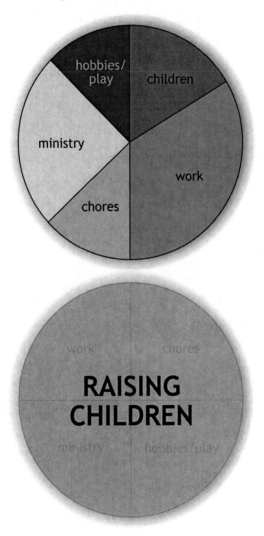

Your children should help you around the house and go with you to do chores, and you should let them watch you in life—how else will they learn? Certainly there are times of sitting down and reading with them or playing with them, but it cannot just be that. Whenever you can, bring them along. This is how we are instructed to teach them all that God has commanded us:

> "Hear, O Israel: The LORD our God, the LORD is one. You shall love the LORD your God with all your heart and with all your soul and with all your might. And these words that I command you today shall be on your heart. You shall teach them diligently to your children, and shall talk of them when you sit in your house, and when you walk by the way, and when you lie down, and when you rise. You shall bind them as a sign on your hand, and they shall be as frontlets between your eyes. You shall write them on the doorposts of your house and on your gates." (Deuteronomy 6:4-9)

This is the foundational text for discipleship in parenting. The Christian life is not compartmentalized from "everyday" life; it saturates and permeates *all* of life—and your parenting does as well. How can we be faithful to this if we aren't there?

The Father sacrificed much for you to be in His presence. As fathers imaging *the* Father, we must sacrifice time with the guys, hunting trips, late hours at work, and time at the golf course so that our children would be anchored—not adrift at sea, being "tossed to and fro by every wave of doctrine" (Eph. 4:14) or every swell the ideas and philosophies of this world ask them to surf in. It is our time, our there-ness, that they need.

REFLECTION QUESTIONS

1. What about God's presence stirs your heart to worship and joy?

2. How are you fulfilling the role as anchor for your kids? Have you abdicated your role and the anchor has become money, school, or amenities?

3. What is God calling you to sacrifice to be present with your family?

4. What activities or errands should you take your children with you on?

CHAPTER TWO

BE GENEROUS WITH YOUR CREATIVITY

"The whole earth is filled with His glory. Every day creation shouts to us, God is glorious! God is creator! God is provider! God is love! God is there!"
— *Steve Dewitt*

MEN SLAVE and toil in their careers, catalyzing new projects, completing tasks, exerting creative energy one rung of the ladder at a time in order to reach the ubiquitous—albeit, intangible and fleeting—goal of "making it," whatever that means. So, home for most husbands and fathers is a sort of glass-housed "man-cave" where they watch sports and chill in full view of a wife and children taking second place to their comforts.

In effect, date nights don't happen with the wife, nor are they creatively planned; time with the children is short, unplanned, perhaps "redundant" and mundane; weekend after weekend, holiday after holiday, vacation after vacation. The boss you don't like, the co-workers you use as the rungs to your "making it" ladder, and the hope of success are the depository of all your creativity and mental energy. You only have so much in that mind reservoir and, well, "I want to make a good life for my family." Sure you do . . .

ℰℛ ℭℛ

The plight of this common man goes much deeper and needs far more work than I have space for here. The deep idols of a man that seeks his identity, worth, and significance in his job must be rooted out by the Gospel so that his work becomes his vocation— or calling—in order to glorify God, work hard and rest hard, and to create culture, goods, and ideas for the common good (see Every Good Endeavor, Tim Keller). What also suffers from this root idolatry and the bad fruit it bears is your family—your wife gets your fumes and your children get your vapors because your work (read, *you*) gets all your high octane fuel.

Thankfully, God does not treat us in the same inverted, selfish way.

"My Father is working until now, and I am working" (John 5:17). Jesus said His Dad is always working, so work can't be a bad thing. But for what purpose is the Father working? In this case, Jesus had just healed a man on the Sabbath—a big no-no in the skewed work policy of the religious elite of Jesus' time. You didn't work on the Sabbath. Jesus worked anyway. His Father works too, always for our good. The wisdom of the Father at work in redemptive history is astounding, and we image the Father when we use the fullness of our creative capacity to love our family.

OUR FATHER'S CREATIVE PLAN FOR US

"Yet among the mature we do impart wisdom, although it is not a wisdom of this age or of the rulers of this age, who are doomed to pass away. But we impart a secret and hidden wisdom of God, which God decreed before the ages for our glory." (1 Corinthians 2:6-7)

The secret and hidden wisdom of God is the full-range creative plan of the Gospel of Jesus to save sinners for the glory of God and the joy of the redeemed. Paul puts this creative, wise plan in its eschatological perspective—eternity past ("before the ages") to eternity future. Like taking a brilliant, faceted jewel, he takes us back to the minerals that formed it over ages and ages to be amazed at the creative plan of the Father for His children.

Imagine this, before anything existed, the Father calls the Son and the Spirit:

> "I am going to create Jim, I have these great things planned for his enjoyment that he might marvel at our works and be complete in his joy. I have oceans, sunsets, baseball, brisket, good music, daughters, and a beautiful wife, all creatively planned for him. Only he is going to want to be his own god, he is going to rebel, he is going to self-rely, and self-glorify, and be self-dependent and selfish—but I love him.
>
> So, Jesus, 2000 years before Jim is born, I want you to die for him, I want you to be a substitutionary, spotless Lamb in order that we might save him. Then, Spirit, a little while after he is born, I want you to explode in his heart the truth and reality of what we are planning today that his heart might soar over the wonders of our work for him, so that all affections for anything

else are displaced by the weight of our glory and the depth of our love. Then I want you to never leave him, daily reminding him of our great love for him."

Are you still breathing?

How generous the Father is with his creativity and wisdom towards you!

❦

I remember I was still sleeping when my wife walked into our bedroom, jumped on the bed next me, woke me up furiously shaking me (I am a very hard sleeper) and shoved the pregnancy test into my face. "Are two blue lines good?" I asked. What a joyous moment! Though, admittedly, having a baby wasn't all that real to me until we heard the heartbeat at the twelve-week appointment, what was real was the planning that needed to be done. The nursery had to be creatively decorated; we needed to find a crib, a changing table, a swing, and everything else a newborn would need. What would we name her? What needs to happen financially? So much wisdom and creativity went into preparing for our little image-bearer who would soon light up our hearts. Why does it end after they are born? How do work and hobbies slip back into the number one spot, exhausting all our creative wisdom and planning?

ALL OF CREATION A GIFT

In his great book, *Meals With Jesus*, Tim Chester observes, "The world is far more delicious than it needs to be." Have you ever thought about how generous God is to us in creation? It seems peculiar to think of the great *creativity* in *creation*, but how easily do days and weeks pass by as we take for granted all the tastes and colors and variety and beauty that the Father has given us in creation? The evolutionist sees creation as perchance, but has there ever been so much beauty that *wasn't* a gift? What is the purpose of the Father's generous and wise creativity?

"Creation speaks to us—every day, all the time, constantly shouting truths about spiritual reality. Did you hear it this morning as you got up? Did you feel any truth about God this morning as you took a hot shower? Did you taste any truth as you delighted in your morning coffee? Did you hear any divine reality as you heard a bird singing? Did you see any truth as you saw the blue of the sky? What have you actually felt, tasted, touched, seen, and heard today? The whole earth is filled with His glory. Every day creation shouts to us, God is glorious! God is creator! God is provider! God is love! God is there! . . . Everywhere I look, everything I feel, hear, smell, and taste transmits the beauty of God through the beauty of creation. He is the beauty behind all beauty."[6]

Our creativity and wisdom to our children are invitations. We invite them into our love for them, into our presence, and we hold their hands as we take them on a tour of all the delights the Father has given His children. Why? We do it that they might see the "beauty behind all beauty," the Creator behind all creation, Wisdom behind all that is wise.

IMAGING THE FATHER'S CREATIVITY & WISDOM

What would it look like to image this great, creative, wise Father who uses His creativity and wisdom for His children?

Do you have dates with your daughter?
Do you create adventures for your son?
Do you build traditions around the holidays for
your new family?

Do you plan for vacations?

Do you save up money—sacrificing golf or hunting or poker—so you can build memories with your kids?

Have you thought and prayed through life insurance, college funds, and other financial legacies you can leave?

Do you do ministry with your children?

Do you take them to serve?

Do you bring them to the hospital to visit someone in your City Group?

Do they see you pray for people?

       ℰ   ℭ

You see, work and money are tools. They are tools for mission. The mission is to make disciples, and your children need to be discipled. You use your work and money to disciple them. A good disciple-maker spends lots of time with those he is discipling. He does everyday life with them; he shares his life and lives openly in front of them so that they might see what it looks like for someone to follow Jesus. A disciple-maker does not work hard at a job so he can afford to send the one he should be discipling to disciple camp, or buy him a book, or worse, not disciple him to Jesus at all. If we outsource the time necessary to disciple our children, we teach them our own skewed view of the world—discipling them to the deep idols that we worship. Because of the Gospel—the secret, hidden wisdom of God decreed before the ages—we are transformed (made a disciple), formed (being discipled), and conformed to the image of God (empowered to make disciples).

A loving father images the loving Father through generously and creatively discipling his children with the full capacity of his knowledge, mental energy, wisdom, and planning. He does all of this for fun with dad, time with dad, memories with dad, laughter with dad, security with dad, and dates with dad. Oh that your children might see your Father's great wisdom and love for them through your generosity! It takes planning, time, and creativity to show them the full breadth of the generous Father. Be generous in everything that their joy may be full (John 16:23-24)!

Our Father is generous in showing us His glory, and we serve our children by showing them His glory as well. We do this by leading them to Jesus, who happens to overflow with the glory of the Father. How do we do that? We do it by delighting in Jesus and, therefore, imaging the Father.

REFLECTION QUESTIONS

1. How does God's generous creativity hit you?
2. Do you have dates with your daughter?
3. Do you create adventures for your son?
4. Do you build traditions around the holidays for your new family?
5. Do you plan for vacations?

CHAPTER THREE

BE GENEROUS WITH YOUR MONEY

"Is there any good thing that the Father has withheld from us?" — *Douglas Wilson*

I NEEDED to repent to my wife. Let me explain. I am freakish about money: budgets, bill pay, saving. I know where every dollar goes. Additionally, I am certain what we should spend money on and what we shouldn't. Money spent on the home that will increase value is good, but furniture and clothes are bad. However, what I value is not the same as what my wife values. She likes clothes (what girl doesn't); she likes furnishings (again, very weird, right?); and, of course, she likes shoes.

Conviction stemmed from a conversation I was having with a dude *I* was discipling — truth spoken from the mouth of a single dude I was supposed to be teaching truth to. I shared with him about a conflict we had over money. I invested in a back patio (Oklahoma flagstone) because we wanted it, but also because it would increase the value of our home — it was an investment. The argument arose from her frustration with my resistance and nit picking over her buying some clothes. To be fair to my girl, she does not shop often and always buys on sale. The person I was discipling gently let me know that I was not valuing what she was valuing, which devalues her.

So I repented. I also practiced the lost art of restitution. I took her on a shopping spree. It was a lot of shoes.

Men lean either to the left or to the right on the "managing money" spectrum: Left, you don't plan well, you spend everything, so you have nothing to give; or to the right, you are freakish, tight-fisted, not fun, boring, and you view money as just security and not also a tool to wield to love your family. Our Father blesses. Our Father gives generously. We should too.

THE FATHER'S GENEROSITY

Imaging the Father through being generous with your money is not just about buying your family stuff. It goes much deeper. It reflects a Father who has given us *literally* everything. The Father gives all that He has, and He has a lot—a cattle on a thousand hills are His (translated: a Mercedes on a thousand car lots).

He gives us His home: "In my Father's house are many rooms. If it were not so, would I have told you that I go to prepare a place for you?" (John 14:2).

He gives us clothes: "Consider the lilies, how they grow: they neither toil nor spin, yet I tell you, even Solomon in all his glory was not arrayed like one of these. But if God so clothes the grass, which is alive in the field today, and tomorrow is thrown into the oven, how much more will he clothe you, O you of little faith!" (Luke 12:27-28).

He gives us food: "Consider the ravens: they neither sow nor reap, they have neither storehouse nor barn, and yet God feeds them. Of how much more value are you than the birds!" (Luke 12:24).

He gives us all things in fact: "So let no one boast in men. For *all things are yours*, whether Paul or Apollos or Cephas or the world or life or death or the present or the future — *all are yours*, and you are Christ's, and Christ is God's" (1 Cor. 3:21-23).

The Father is the fountain of all good things, and He generously pours out to His children. As Douglas Wilson asks, "Is there any good thing that the Father has withheld from us?" No.

As prodigal sons, we have already squandered all that He has given us and are in His debt; yet, He set aside the record of debt that was held against us, nailing it to the cross (Col. 2:14). His generosity in the Gospel is such that Paul uses economic language to describe the richness of the Father and our poverty: ". . . though he was rich, yet for your sake he became poor, so that you by his poverty might become rich" (2 Cor. 8:9).

GENEROSITY MODELED

My father modeled generosity. I know this because at least a dozen times my family or friends were generous to me, and they told me why: "Your parents were good to us." I saw my mom write a check every week to the church and put it in the offering plate; we had people live with us almost constantly; they were hospitable, people were always over; they helped those in need. Their money was not their money, it was the Father's.

What are you teaching your children if you value savings and tight-handedness over generosity? Is this a servant posture, or are you just perpetuating the selfishness already flourishing in their hearts? Fostering our children's faith in the Father's providence means not instilling a false hope in money. On the other hand, your children seeing that money is a tool to love people instead of people being a tool to love money teaches them how the Father uses His riches to love us.

℘ ℭ

Every parent experiences the same opportunity to teach our children the generosity of the Father: Sharing. "We need to share, honey." Why? How effective are your words if they don't see you "share" the things your Father has given you? We share because we are given so much. We share because nothing is ultimately ours, but His, and it is lavished on us for our joy and is to be stewarded for the good of others. How can you demand your children to share if you don't? That just makes you a Pharisee: "The . . . Pharisees . . . preach, but do not practice. They tie up heavy burdens, hard to bear, and lay them on people's shoulders, but they themselves are not willing to move them with their finger" (Matt. 23:2-4). Your child's heart is innately selfish, as is yours. It is right for you to teach them to share, but it is pharisaical of you to not show them *how*.

What if they observed mommy and daddy giving gifts or being hospitable? What if your exhortation to them to share is undergirded by your example: "Honey, do you remember when you went with daddy to bring food to the Smiths? We love them and want to give them our stuff. And daddy loves you, that's why he gives you things. And God loves us and gives us so much! So we want to share our things with Johnny just like that. Will you share with Johnny like God shares His toys with us?"

If the goal of parenting is discipleship—rightly imaging God—then we need to raise our children to be generous. As with any discipleship process, we have to show them how. As Spurgeon said, "'Train up a child in the way that he should go', just make sure you go with them!"

IMAGING A RICH GOD WHEN YOU ARE POOR

I said earlier that this is not about buying your family stuff. It does go deeper than that. What do you gain by the Father's generosity?

His providence? Provide for your children. Show them their value and your love by working hard for them, managing your finances well, not going into debt, and living below your means so that spontaneous spending can occur. This could be an unplanned vacation or a drive to your local 7-11 for a Slo-Poke and a Slurpee.

His affections? Love them tangibly with well thought-out gifts. Buy your daughter a new dress and then take her out to a nice restaurant. (You should be her first—and 40th—date. Do not let some 17-year-old punk be the first one to buy her flowers.) Buy your son a new baseball cap and take him to the game.

His thoughts toward you? Don't let them believe they place a distant second to your golfing buddies or your stamp collection or your hunting obsession— you think about them and budget for them. What you buy and how much you spend is inconsequential, it is your heart towards them that matters.

The Father's heart toward us is not just to give us what we need to get by. It is to *lavish* us. He doesn't just give us enough grace to save us, He gives to us generously: " . . . according to the riches of his grace, which he *lavished* upon us" (Eph. 1:7b-8a).

Money is not your children's security, you are. So give to them richly of your time, your grace, *and* your money—whatever tax bracket you are in.

REFLECTION QUESTIONS

1. What moves you from looking at God's generous giving?

2. Do you tend to use people to love money or use money to love people?

3. How can you generously lavish your children?

PART TWO

YOUR FATHER IS GENTLE

"Children are weak and tender creatures, and, as such, they need patient and considerate treatment. We must handle them delicately, like frail machines. They are like young plants, and need gentle watering,—often, but little at a time."
— J.C. Ryle

THE ONLY way to be gentle is to be strong. See, it takes a man—a strong man—to gently respond to someone's anger; you are not swayed or moved emotionally or irrationally to the futile attempts of control from a weaker (sinning) man. It takes a man to gently rebuke his wife when she is in sin; you are not so insecure (weak) that her possible displeasure in you for the rebuke crushes you because you must have her approval. Or, you are gentle and you don't rebuke her in judgement or anger because you are secure (strong) enough in Christ's righteousness that you don't always have to be right. It takes strength to be gentle.

There should be a Vito Corleone-like disposition to you because you are unfazed by others. The Godfather was this way because of his power; you are too because of Christ's rule and reign over everything—ultimate power, strength that is yours in Christ.

God is "slow to anger" and He has "steadfast love," which are patient character traits of an immutable, impassable, strong God. God is immutable—unchanging. His character has never had to grow, He never went through a season of trial that built his character. He always was, always is, and always will be.

In addition, He is impassable—meaning He is not swayed in His emotions, nor does He react or fly off the handle. This is not to say He is emotionless, because He expresses the full range of human emotions (where else did we get them?). The scriptures speak of God's anger (it is righteous and slow), we can grieve the Holy Spirit, and things bring God joy and pleasure. He is peaceful, He is patient, and He is kind. He is everything mentioned in the "love chapter" of 1 Corinthians 13 and everything mentioned in the "fruit of the Spirit" verse in Galatians 5. He *expresses* emotion, but He is not swayed by His emotions. There is nothing that we could do that would change Him or make Him act on his emotions.

So, His meekness and gentleness are tied up in His strength and His power. His sovereign rule and reign is tied up in His kindness, and His kindness leads us to repentance (Rom. 2:4). Our Father is strong *and* gentle. We are to be gentle—in our strength—for our children as well.

CHAPTER FOUR

BE GENTLE TO THEIR MOTHER

"Husbands, live with your wives in an understanding way." — 1 Peter 3:7

WHAT BETTER way to model kindness and gentleness to your children than to be gentle to their mother? 1 Peter 3:7a tells us to "live with [her] in an understanding way." When we are gentle to their mother, we teach our daughters what kind of man to look for and our sons what kind of man to be. Furthermore, we teach both what kind of Heavenly Father they have.

Jesus was (and is) gentle to His Bride, the Church. Jesus doesn't respond to His Bride harshly, but woos her and sacrifices for her, washing her with the water of the word, presenting her to Himself without spot or wrinkle. He is tender to her. In addition, because He is gentle, we see how we are to treat the Church. His example convicts us when we do not love the Church, and it shows us how to.

In the same way, our gentleness to our wives becomes a type of heralding of the Gospel to our children—part of their discipleship. It is as if you are sending the message, "This is how Jesus is to you; this is how He responds to you, speaks to you, and is tender to you!"

THE THEATER OF CONFLICT

Our disagreements with our wives should be done in front of our children. No, not always; sometimes it is wise not to if it is a big argument that may take some time. However, the normal, garden-variety, marital squabbles should be done in their presence. They need to see that disagreements do not separate us; that sin does not get you kicked out of community, but grace draws you nearer to one another. They need to see you, literally, kiss and make up. Your gentleness to their mother in her sin, or in response to yours, shows them how Gospel-formed disciples treat one another in conflict.

Conflict resolution is a skill our children need to learn just as much as math or science or cleaning their room. The Christian life is a communal life because we image a communal, Triune God. If our hope for our children is that they would be able to move from surface-level relationships to deep, grace-centered, iron-sharpening-iron Christian community, then they need to see how violent metal hitting metal is, *and* how gentle grace upon grace can be.

⁊ ⳩

Marriage is difficult and friendships are hard— real ones anyway. While mothers'-day-outs are great, and play dates are helpful, what will teach our children the most about relationships is how we interact with our wives on a day-to-day basis. Conflict is ubiquitous in any close relationship because sin pervades our hearts and is easily awakened from a very light sleep in intimate relationships like marriage. What better teaching moment for our children than to be seated in the audience in the theater of marriage conflict? How will it end? One actor stomping off stage? Will he remember his lines? ("That he might sanctify her, having cleansed her by the washing of water with the word.") Will she remember hers? ("Wives, submit to your own husbands, as to the Lord.") Is this play a tragedy? Or a comedy? Looking back, aren't many of our fights pretty funny?

If our children only see our marriage relationship when it is good—or worse, when we put the mask on and pretend it is—they won't know what to do when a relationship they have goes bad.

ABK: ALWAYS BE KISSING

Public displays of affection (PDA) gross some folks out. In my opinion, they are biblical. Isn't Jesus public about His love for His Bride? Doesn't He tell us that the greatest apologetic to the Gospel is our love for one another (John 13:35)? Wherever you land on the spectrum of PDA—"Gag me" or "How sweet!"—we must see the home as a place to show our children healthy affection. Your boys need to see your tenderness, your pursuit, and your affection for your bride—how else will they learn? The internet? As well, your daughters need to see that affection is good and healthy in marriage, and only in marriage! (Take a moment to remember to clean your guns, men.)

Please kiss your wife in front of your kids often. Kiss her first. Kiss them. Kiss her last. ABK: Always

Be Kissing. Hold her hand. Cuddle with her on the couch during Family Movie Night. Pat her bottom and kiss her neck. Hug. Our Redemption Group ministry is full of men and women who have only seen and experienced unhealthy, sinful affection. Yet, our Father has given us a great gift in sexual intimacy, and, in fact, a *command* to be intimate (1 Cor. 7:5). How will they learn? A book and one conversation about the birds and the bees will not suffice. It must be *multiple* conversations and examples of how a healthy, godly, affectionate marital relationship functions.

FIRST PLACE

Be gentle to their mother *first*. Your children are, by their very nature, selfish, self-centered, self-relying, and self-glorifying. Their default is *self*. Many marriages end in divorce right about the time the youngest child graduates college. Why? Because the marriage was centered on their children, and not each other and Christ. If the family revolves around the children and not the love of mom and dad for each other as a reflection of the Gospel (see Eph. 5:22-33, in particular verse 32), then we only massage the selfishness in them.

We serve our children by serving their mother first. The book of Proverbs, written by a father to his son, implicitly shows the partnership of a father and mother in parenting:

> "A wise son makes a glad father,
> but a foolish son is a sorrow to his mother."
> (Proverbs 10:1)

> "A wise son makes a glad father,
> but a foolish man despises his mother."
> (Proverbs 15:20)

> "Let your father and mother be glad;
> let her who bore you rejoice." (Proverbs 23:25)

Because of the "oneness" in marriage, it is the husband/father's duty to "nourish and cherish" his wife first, for the sake of their children (Eph. 5:28-29).

Fathers, "love your wives, as Christ loved the church and gave himself up for her . . ." (Eph. 5:25). The marriage relationship is a great picture of the Gospel, and your children need to look at that picture often.

REFLECTION QUESTIONS

1. How has God been gentle and grace-filled towards you? How can you extend that same gentleness practically to your wife?

2. Do you tend to hide conflicts with your wife from your children? Will they have a skewed view of relationships because their portrait of life is glossy and fake?

3. If your wife is first, how can you serve her before your children? How can you show her love and grace before your children?

CHAPTER FIVE

BE GENTLE IN RESPONSE TO THEIR FEELINGS

"Fathers, do not provoke your children,
lest they become discouraged."
— Colossians 3:21

"DON'T BE a baby!" What? What sort of moronic parent says something so foolish? The truth is, most parents have or will say something to that affect to their two or three-year old—I know I have. This is a sin. It stems from a fundamental misunderstanding of who our Father is. God is not some distant, cosmic deity that stays separated from our feelings and emotions, our hurts and sorrows, and our trials and sufferings. No, God draws near. Hebrews 2:18 says that Jesus suffered in every way that we do—even in the suffering a two-year-old faces. Let us not forget that at one point Jesus was a two-year-old!

The incarnation of God shows the heart of the Father that sent the Son: A heart to enter in, a heart to know, a heart to sympathize. *He knows!* [7]

> He knows the pain from the betrayal of a friend.[a]
> He knows the heartache of friends who aren't there in times of need.[b]
> He knows the hardships of financial strife.[c]
> He knows the abandonment of familial division.[d]
> He knows the pain of suffering.[e]
> He knows what it is like to be tired.[f]
> He knows what it is like to be tempted.[g]
> He knows what it is like to be misunderstood.[h]

If the God of the universe can enter into our suffering, understand our emotions, and sympathize with our feelings, then shouldn't we do the same with our children?

> Don't you know what it is like to not get what you want?
> Don't you know what it is like to be tired? Or hungry?

Don't you know what it is like to want attention?

Don't you know what it is like to want everything
to cater to you?

Haven't you felt like your Father is robbing you
of joy?

Haven't you felt like your Dad took something
from you too soon?

Haven't you felt like God was against you at
times?

I promise you, nothing your child feels, nor the
way in which they respond to that feeling, is foreign to
you. *You know!*

So why, if we know, if we can sympathize, do we
not enter in? At the heart of such a moronic response to
our kids, "Don't be a baby!" is selfishness. ("Don't be a
baby" has cousins: "Stop whining!"; "Grow up!"; "Stop
crying!"; "Don't be a brat"; or worse, we just ignore them.)
At that point, whether we say it or just think it, we are
choosing ourselves over this young, little one who bears
our image. We are inconvenienced by their outburst.
Their desires are robbing our desire for comfort or quiet
or an obedient child. Our retort of "Don't be a baby!" *is
no different from the outburst* that fueled ours, and neither
is the heart motivation behind it. We want something

and they want something, and those somethings are now competing. Who wins? As parents, we will always win that battle. Yet, the very message of the Gospel is that God will lose for us, He chose us —His image-bearers (Gen. 1:28)—over His very own life.

An understanding of God's response to you changes you.

Harper (my two-year-old) sometimes has a conniption when she doesn't get her way. My response goes one of two ways: 1) The moronic, selfish response of a grown man that forgets the Gospel and forgets who my Father is, or 2) A sympathetic understanding and acknowledgment that I have conniptions when I don't get my way too. Now I am at her level, we are on an even playing field—we are both sinners. I can squat down and say, "I know honey, I know how you feel." I can respond gently and speak truth in love. It is the difference between provoking them (tempting them further to sin) and loving them as our Father loves us.

GRACIOUS LOVE, NOT PROVOCATION

> "Fathers, *do not provoke* your children, lest they become discouraged." (Colossians 3:21)

> "Fathers, *do not provoke* your children to anger . . ." (Ephesians 6:8)

Our desires or emotions are typically good, godly desires that sin robs and twists into selfishness, tantrums (the child or adult kind), and an entitled heart. Like the Israelites who demanded manna, we demand from God good things like food, love, affection, affirmation, and joy. However, we either already have these things in Him, or they are things He would gladly give us. Likewise, our children demand manna from us instead of just asking.

They want attention; they throw the milk on the ground. They want affection; they hit their sister. They want food; they disobey and climb on the counter to get it. Total depravity is a heart condition that even a two-year-old suffers from, and it is provocation enough—a father works *against* his child and not *for* his child when he joins in the provoking.

How do we work *for* our child in the midst of their selfish desires?

"A *soft answer* turns away wrath,
    but a harsh word stirs up anger.

The *tongue of the wise* commends knowledge,
    but the mouths of fools pour out folly.

A *gentle tongue* is a tree of life,
    but perverseness in it breaks the spirit."
    (Proverbs 15:1-2, 4)

A soft answer. A wise word. A gentle tongue. Is this not how our Father responds to us?

> "Therefore, behold, I will allure her,
>   and bring her into the wilderness,
>   and speak tenderly to her."
> (Hosea 2:14)

In the great story of Hosea, we are Gomer, the prostitute. We have godly desires that we seek to satisfy in ungodly ways. We continually go back to idols, selling our bodies as we pour out time, money, and energy for things that *promise* to satiate, but still leave us thirsty. Like a toddler that wants more and more and more, we want more of what has never satisfied. When our God won't give us our god, we throw a tantrum.

Our Father responds to us, not as an annoyed Father fed up with the sensitive feelings of an ungrateful people, but with a gracious love that is more appealing than any additional cookie, a box of crackers, a toy, a new job, more money, or whatever earthly desire we are coveting.

He *allures* us. It is the face of a loving Father, the countenance of a patient, strong, gracious Daddy who gently kneels down to get at our level (remember,

Jesus came down!). In the same way, my wife and I try to gently, calmly, and lovingly embrace and respond to our paroxysmal daughter. Our face is not conveying ire, but love. *A soft answer.*

He *brings us into the wilderness*. He leads us out of temptation. He leads us into His presence. He is peace (Eph. 2:14). He is love (1 John 4:8). Now we are in the presence of Peace and Love. Often, immediately after a tantrum, I will take Harper into her room and say, "Let's talk, honey." Sometimes, in the middle, I discipline her, but it always ends and begins the same way: It ends with a kiss and an embrace. It begins with me explaining to her why we shouldn't respond in that way when we don't get what we want. How we have so much. That more of what she wants could hurt her. I am not trying to rob her of joy but be a force-shield for anything that would try to do so. *A wise word.*

He *speaks tenderly to us*. How can He do this? How can a holy, righteous God not light us up for our constant rebellion, our continual transgressions? He can because His love is patient. It is called *steadfast love*. The Jesus Storybook Bible calls the Father's steadfast love His, "Never Stopping, Never Giving Up, Unbreaking, Always and Forever Love." As well, I want to speak tenderly to my daughter—not assuaging her conniption and selfishness, but tenderly and lovingly speaking truth to her. *A gentle tongue.*

℘ ℭ

Any parent can tell you how difficult this is. Often, though, the reason given is insufficient—partially true—but insufficient nonetheless. It is *not* difficult primarily because children don't listen and are so rebellious, but because we don't know the love of the Father toward us in our feelings. We get angry. We get discouraged. However, it can't be the Father who is provoking us to that. Look again at the instruction Paul gives fathers:

> "Fathers, do not provoke your children, *lest they become discouraged.*" (Colossians 3:21)

> "Fathers, do not provoke your children to *anger . . .*" (Ephesians 6:8)

Obviously, God wouldn't instruct us not to do something that He does. So, what leads to our discouragement and anger? Our sin. In the same vein, our children are already susceptible to discouragement and anger because of sin—it is in their hearts, and their sin can be turned up at that drop of a hat (or a resounding "No!" from you). Our calling as parents is not to provoke or *tempt* them to sin, but to show them their need for a Savior.

If we do not respond gently then we are, again, like Pharisees. In Matthew 23, after Jesus says that they tie up heavy burdens on people and don't lift a finger to help, He says this:

> "But woe to you, scribes and Pharisees, hypocrites! For *you shut the kingdom of heaven in people's faces.* For you neither enter yourselves nor allow those who would enter to go in. Woe to you, scribes and Pharisees, hypocrites! For you travel across sea and land to make a single proselyte, and when he becomes a proselyte, *you make him twice as much a child of hell as yourselves.*" (Matthew 23:13-15)

This is a strong word, certainly, but I believe it is fitting. As parents we are called to lead our children to the Lord; we are to *open* the kingdom of heaven to them. We do this by imaging the Father, showing them their need for a Savior, and not provoking them *to* sin, but instead leading them *from* sin into the Father's presence.

Let the gentle response of your Father change you. Let His alluring and wooing, His soft answer and gentle tongue, lead you to repentance and change. As Paul Tripp has said, "If I were ever to be the tool of transforming grace in the lives of my children, I needed to be daily rescued, not from them, but from me!"[8]

REFLECTION QUESTIONS

1. How does God pursue you when you rebel from His truth, reject His work on your behalf, and run from His glory?

2. How have you responded to your children selfishly?

3. Is the Holy Spirit convicting you of any sin that you need to repent of to God, your wife, and/or children?

4. By God's grace, and the power of the Holy Spirit, how can you respond to your children with a soft answer, a wise word, and a gentle tongue?

CHAPTER SIX

BE GENTLE
IN RESPONSE TO
THEIR SIN

*"Or do you . . . not know that God's kindness is meant to
lead you to repentance?"*
— *Romans 2:3-4*

WE MUST respond to sin. We distort the image of who God is if we are lazy in our discipline of our children. God hates sin. He hates the sin of your child. Your child was conceived in sin (Ps. 51:5). From conception, your daughter's heart was bent away from God; your son is dead spiritually until the Holy Spirit breathes life into him and gives him a new heart (Eph. 2:1; Ez. 36:26). Sin demands a response. We are called to push back darkness, and darkness resides in your little one's heart—do not minimize their sin ("She's tired"); do not excuse them ("They are so young"); do not disregard it ("I'm too tired to address this"). That is unloving to your child and dishonoring to God—we must respond to sin.

Yet, it is God's gentleness, or kindness, that leads to our repentance:

> "Do you suppose, O man . . . that you will escape the judgment of God? Or do you presume on the riches of his kindness and forbearance and patience, not knowing that God's kindness is meant to lead you to repentance?" (Romans 2:3-4)

God is patient and kind in response to our sin. The father in the Prodigal Son parable "entreats" the older brother to come inside to the party. He pleads with him, and his eyes are insisting, inviting, "come in!"

> ". . . He was angry and refused to go in. His father came out and *entreated him*." (Luke 15:28)

This is how fathers should respond in gentleness to their children's sin, by inviting them to repentance. Begrudging obedience is not the goal: the goal is freedom. It is trust; it is joy; it is protection; it is security.

Do you grab your son's arm roughly? Do you raise your voice? Do you get frustrated but think, somehow, that it is not seeping through in your tone or pouring out in your look?

Do you give them *that look*, the look that says, "you-better-stop-right-now-or-else"? Do you imagine your Father looks at you look like that?

UNMOVING & MOVING

In 1 Corinthians chapter 13, the famous love chapter, Paul couples the Father's patience (steadfastness) and kindness again when describing what biblical love would look like if it were personified:

"Love is patient and kind . . ." (1 Corinthians 13:4a)

The Father is gentle in his response to our rebellion, and gentle in His pursuit of our hearts in our sin.

This kind of love in response to sin is both *unmoved* and *moving*. Picture the Father standing, immovable, with everything around Him warring and rebelling against Him, mocking Him: shaking fists, contemptuous looks, frustrated gestures—yet His love standing fierce, rock solid, and unchanged. At the same time, He is moving *toward His children as they rebel*. His kind and gentle love is not a doormat.

It pursues. It is a relentless pursuit. It reaches for; it embraces; it chases after. When the kindness of the Father pursues you, and eventually collides with your rebellious heart, it changes you—it leads you to repentance.

Let us take a look at this unmoved, yet moving gentle kindness. How can we be gentle and kind as we pursue our children in their sin? How does our gentle kindness lead them to change? How can we take an active, not defensive, posture in their sin?

A GENTLE PURSUIT

Passivity permeates all sons of Adam and is the default setting of our now distorted image of the Father. The Father is not passive. However, our father, Adam, was:

> "So when the woman saw that the tree was good for food . . . she took of its fruit and ate, and she also gave some to her husband who *was with her*, and he ate." (Genesis 3:6)

Attacked and deceived, Eve succumbs to her desires and sins. Where was her husband? He was right next to her *doing nothing*. I am convinced man's greatest sin is passivity. In church culture, we tend to focus a lot on what *not* to do—don't have sex, don't lie, don't steal. "Don't drink or smoke or chew, or go with girls who do." The result is that nice church boys are celebrated, patted on the back, and, often, sent to seminary to be trained in the pastorate because they *don't do* bad things. What *do* they do, though?

Isn't passivity just as bad? Are not sins of *omission* just as depraved as sins of *commission*? My wife and I have counseled dozens of couples entering marriage, and by far the biggest issue we have seen with the men is what they *don't do*, not what they do that they shouldn't.

Is not your child's sin a big deal? If they continue in it, will they not forever be separated from God in hell? Does their sin not rob them of joy just as your sin robs you of your joy? Our Father sees sin as a huge deal. From before the foundations of the earth, He had a plan to deal with the sin issue:

> ". . . knowing that you were ransomed from the futile ways inherited from your forefathers, not with perishable things such as silver or gold, but with the precious blood of Christ . . . *He was foreknown before the foundation of the world* but was made manifest in the last times for the sake of you who through him are believers in God . . ." (1 Peter 1:18-21a)

Our Father's gentle pursuit of us originated prior to creation. That is one long and patient journey to deal with our rebellious hearts. He is not passive.

We cannot be lazy in our children's sin. How? First, draw near to them. Don't yell from across the room. Don't ignore it. Don't make a passive aggressive comment, "Oh, you have such a hard life, no more cookies, what great suffering you are going through!" Draw near. Furthermore, call sin what it is—sin. "You disobeyed daddy, honey. That is a sin." Love is willing to pursue, and it does so gently. As the hymn, "In Tenderness," sings:

> "*In tenderness He sought me,*
> *Weary and sick with sin,*
> And on His shoulders brought me
> Back to His fold again."[9]

GENTLENESS THAT TRANSFORMS

"Harper, why would you do that!" Milk is now everywhere. Why are we surprised at our children's sin? Further, why are we surprised that *we* don't have the power to change them? This is what Paul Tripp began to see: "I began to realize that as a parent I had not been called to be the producer of change, but to be a willing tool in the powerful hands of a God who alone has the power and willingness to undo us and rebuild us again."[10]

We are tools, shadows of the Father, reflectors of His gentle kindness in sin. If His "kindness leads us to repentance," then our frustration, our law, and even our discipline will have no effect on their hard hearts.

What is our hope then? Why worry about loving-kindness? Why try to image the gentle response of the Father in our sin to our children?

> "For this is why the gospel was preached even to those who are dead, that though judged in the flesh the way people are, they might live in the spirit the way God does . . . Above all, keep loving one another earnestly, *since love covers a multitude of sins.*" (1 Peter 4:6,8)

We preach the Gospel to our children when we respond in kindness to their sin, never excusing it, but not lashing out against it. We share with them the kindness the Father has shown us, we join them in the fight against their sin that the Father will win with His grace and kindness towards them in Christ. *This* is our only hope for our children.

NOT DEFENSIVE, BUT GENTLE POSTURE

The Father does not take a defensive posture towards us. Rather, He is on the offensive. Too many times we respond passively by either ignoring our children's sin or being passive aggressive in it. We take their disobedience personally. Again, Tripp is helpful:

> "As a father, I too often live for comfort, appreciation, success, respect, and control. None of those things, in and of themselves, is wrong. But they must not rule my heart. If they do rule my heart, then in a moment of [my child's sin], *I will likely personalize what is not personal* and be adversarial in my approach to them. At that moment, I will be enraged because [my child] has stopped me from doing or having what I really most want. I'll settle for a quick solution because I just want to get it over with. I'll turn a moment of God-given ministry opportunity into a moment of anger. I won't see how to wisely *go towards* his heart."[11]

When we are defensive in response to our children's sin, we work inversely to how the Father responds to us. God is *unmoved*—love unchanging, not taking our sin personally and responding out of frustration. And He is also *moving*—going towards our hearts, gently, kindly pursuing us.

Sin demands a response. A godly father's response is gentle. It will only be gentle if he has experienced the loving pursuit of a strong Father in his own sin.

"The sin, weakness, rebellion, or failure of your children is never an imposition on your parenting. It is never an interruption. It is never a hassle. It is always grace. And because in these moments He asks you to forsake your agenda for His, this opportunity of grace is not just for your children, it's for you as well."[12]

REFLECTION QUESTIONS

1. As you reflect on God's patient and kind love toward you, what emotions or thoughts arise?

2. How can you extend God's patient and kind love with your children?

3. Do you tend to take your children's sin personally or respond out of frustration?

4. How will you pursue your children in their sin as God pursued you?

PART THREE

YOUR FATHER
IS GRACIOUS

"Where sin increased, grace abounded all the more." —
Apostle Paul

G RACE IS spoken of with relative ease in
Evangelical circles. As much as the word "Gospel"
is thrown around, so too is "grace;" yet, I wonder if we
really understand the weight of the word, the depth in
it, or what it *really* constitutes.

Grace sounds so sweet, doesn't it? The word
conjures up images of a doe, perhaps a ballerina, or, in
the context of Christianity, maybe a nice, benevolent
deity who showers us with love and sort of laughs off
our rebellion like many parents do when their children

disobey them: "Oh, Johnny, you silly boy, don't pull your sister's hair, [ha ha, giggle giggle]."

The grace of God is not like this. Just a cursory reading of the New Testament reveals the power and depth of grace, but it is perhaps most evident in the first two chapters of Ephesians. There we see that grace originates from "God the Father" (1:2), that the Father's love for us—His adopted sons (1:5)—since before oceans and stars were created, *terminates* with us praising this "glorious grace" (1:6), and that we have been redeemed "through his blood . . . according to the riches of his grace" (1:7).

Grace comes from the Father.
Grace enables sons to praise the Father's glory.
Grace bleeds out.

As well, though we were dead—no spiritual heartbeat, no life, no breath—the Father "made us alive together with [the Son], by *grace* you have been saved" (2:5). Eternity is needed for us to swim the depths of the Father's "immeasurable riches of grace" that have drowned all of our sin (2:7). We have been given grace—not because of great works we have done, not because we deserved it—but as a "gift of God [the Father]" (2:8).

Grace makes dead things alive.
Grace drowns sin and is eternally deep.
Grace is a gift from the Father to His sons.

Grace is not cute and sweet. Grace is God on a tree—a bloody cross and an empty tomb. Grace is costly for the giver, but free for the recipient. Grace will tear you apart, and then put you back together. Biblical grace is powerful.

§§§ §§§

You cannot change your child's heart. The only hope your children have is to experience the grace of the Father. Your desire should be that your children experience the same grace you are experiencing. This means, as Elyse Fitzpatrick says, "Parenting is partnering."[13] We are to partner with our children, walk with them, showing them their need for grace by showing them *your* need for grace and by *imaging* the Father's grace to them. What are your other options?

Your intimidation, your threats, your raised voice, even your biblical discipline, your family devotionals, and your religious activities can do nothing to change your children—they are dead spiritually (Eph. 2:1). In the first half of Romans, the Apostle Paul juxtaposes the Law and the Gospel, showing that the Law was powerless to change us:

> "Now the law came in to increase the trespass, but where sin increased, grace abounded all the more, so that, as sin reigned in death, grace also might reign through righteousness leading to eternal life through Jesus Christ our Lord." (Romans 5:20–21)

When we try to image the Law, and not the grace of God, we exasperate our children. We are not good law-givers. As Paul Tripp says, "The law changes everyday, some days I am tolerant, others I am less so. Our children, then, have to be emotional weathermen, 'What's dad's temperature today?'"[14] Even if we were perfect in our law-giving, it would just "increase the trespass," acting as a mirror to condemn our children because they are unable to meet the law's requirements.

The only hope, therefore, is that we would lavish the same grace the Father has given us on our children, partnering with them, unsurprised by their sin, standing ready to extend grace—the same grace we have received.

CHAPTER SEVEN

BE GRACIOUS IN THEIR SIN

*"And [the prodigal son] arose and came to his father.
But while he was still a long way off, his father saw him
and felt compassion, and ran and embraced him and
kissed him."*
— *Luke 15:20*

WHEN PEOPLE sin against us, we lose sight of the vertical nature of sin (a sin is ultimately against God) and only see it horizontally, or personally. We are offended, and we think, "How dare they? Don't they know who I am?" Immediately, their ability to affirm our greatness is diminished, thus we remove our love and affection for them, revealing what we truly valued them for. They are of less use to us now, as if the relationship was of a utilitarian nature (useful in affirming our greatness) rather than mutual submission—leading each other to the Son (Eph. 5:21). Therefore, we withdraw. Nice.

This does not change when it comes to our relationships with our children. I found myself intrinsically, innately, unconsciously wanting to withhold my love from my oldest daughter when she would disobey me. I wanted to physically distance myself from her, not drawing her near to me in her sin, but pushing her away. I wanted to emotionally distance myself from her, embracing the offense in my selfish heart and the anger that accompanies all sin towards my prideful heart. This is not at all how our Father responds to our sin.

God, in his grace, draws near in our sin. In our rebellion, we scamper away towards our limited delights only to find them empty and unfulfilling, distancing ourselves from the limitless delights of God with every skip away from Him and closer to his stuff. It is the same song and dance my Harper does sometimes when she disobeys daddy: She runs away, going to the farthest point in the room, not looking at me, sometimes with a sly look, sometimes a guilty frown.

All of it is just distance, it is separation. She is happiest, safest, and most secure when she is abiding in daddy; sin robs her of that. The law written on her heart condemns her and she responds like any good, little midget Pharisee with pride ("no!") or despair (picture the cutest possible curly-haired Pharisee, furrowed brow, frowning face, lip doubled over). We do the same thing—it is the adult version and not as cute, but the same nonetheless. Yet, the Father, in His grace, runs towards us like the dad in the Prodigal Son parable— hiked up robe, shameless sprint, running hard after us. It is enough to soften any heart. It is irresistible grace.

LIKE ISRAEL, LIKE CHILDREN

The Israelites were like little children. They complained about being hungry after God threw the Red Sea waters aside like a rag doll in order to save their hind parts from the Egyptian army. Then they grumbled when they got tired of the food God gave them, which was the chef special to end all chef specials—manna falling from heaven. "Oh, my bad, you didn't like the miracle food I dropped from Jupiter for you?"

Despite their childish tantrums, the grace of God towards them was thrilling. Aside from the plagues to destroy their enemies, the Red Sea rag-doll toss, and the miracle food, God's purpose for delivering them is what really amazes me:

> "Say therefore to the people of Israel, 'I am the LORD, and I will bring you out from under the burdens of the Egyptians, and I will deliver you from slavery to them, and I will redeem you . . . *I will take you to be my people, and I will be your God* . . ." (Exodus 6:6-7)

God delivers His people *out* of bondage and slavery to bring them *in* to His presence to be their God. In the same way, the Son redeems us in order to reconcile us to the Father so that we might be in His presence. Further, our goal for our children in their slavery to sin is that they would be in our presence—not distant from us, far from us, or separated from us, but near us. We cannot compound their default to separate in their sin by distancing ourselves from them. That is a sinful response to sin that we inherit from an earthly father, and it does not image God *the* Father.

LIKE ADAM & EVE, LIKE CHILDREN

Sin by its very nature separates, divides, and isolates. We see this immediately in the first sinners, our parents, Adam and Eve. After our first parents sinned, they did what every two-year-old (and adult) does—they hid:

> "And they heard the sound of the LORD God walking in the garden in the cool of the day, and *the man and his wife hid themselves from the presence of the LORD God* among the trees of the garden." (Genesis 3:8)

My little Harper is just doing what her mother Eve did long ago. She is "suppressing the truth" (Romans 1:18). Our children hide and distance themselves because of guilt, shame, and pride. They shout, "no!" out of a rebellious heart conditioned to be autonomous in their decision-making as opposed to being submissive as the Son is to His loving Father— doing everything just as He asks:

> "So Jesus said to them, "Truly, truly, I say to you, the Son can do nothing of his own accord, but only what he sees the Father doing. *For whatever the Father does, that the Son does likewise.* For the Father loves the Son and shows him all that he himself is doing . . . I can do nothing on my own. As I hear, I judge, and my judgment is just, *because I seek not my own will but the will of him who sent me.*" (John 5:19-20a, 30)

We should not expect our children to respond to their sin with righteousness, but with more sin as they walk further and further away. Jesus was the only perfect Son; He alone obeys the Father perfectly. Our sons (and daughters) need the Son, and we should show them that need—that is godly parenting.

So, how do *we* respond to their sin? Our children, like Adam and Eve (and like us!), respond to sin by hiding, so what should our response be? It should be like the Father's:

> "But the LORD God called to the man and said to him, 'Where are you?'" (Genesis 3:9)

God comes after them! He pursues them, looks for them, and calls out to them, "Where are you?" This is grace. Grace pursues. It goes after. It chases. It asks, lovingly, "Where are you?"

Furthermore, godly grace takes a beating. It is a beating to deal with your child's sin day after day, week after week. It is a melee of sin when you have children; each new depraved heart you add to your quiver adds exponentially to the wallops you take as little sinner after little sinner takes a turn at you. As the authority, you are the target, and you are going to get hit.

Is your child sinning against you by disobeying you? Absolutely. Imaging God means you wear it—you do not minimize it, you do not excuse it—you wear it. Take the beating and pursue. Do not distance yourself from them or withdraw your love and affection, but pour out even more. This is the Father's love to us, a grace-drenched, infinite-pursuit, even in our sin.

"But they are so disobedient!"

"They don't appreciate me and they disobey!"

I know. Our sin runs deep. But grace runs deeper. Grace drowns sin.

A GRACIOUS PURSUIT

We see God pursuing Adam and Eve, and we see Him desire to deliver the Israelites out of slavery and into His presence. However, the most evidentiary reality of the pursuit of the Gracious Father bursts forth in the giving of His Son. Jesus tabernacled, He "tented" with us, that is how near He drew, even in our sin (John 1:14). He breathed our air, ate our food, touched our lepers, ate with our prostitutes, loved our self-righteous, and died our death. Because of the Son, we have the Father.

Have you thought deeply on what the incarnation of Jesus must mean? Think of billions and billions of children all disobeying, all inching towards the farthest point of the room, getting as far away from the Father as possible, responding in pride:

"There is no God!"
"I don't need you!"
"Either stay out of my way or help me get what I want!"

Or despair:

"Where were you when . . . ?"
"I must not be able to make you happy."
"I guess I need to do more."

What a beating God has to take!
Does God ever get frustrated with you?

> "The LORD, the LORD, a God merciful and gracious, *slow to anger, and abounding in steadfast love and faithfulness . . .*" (Exodus 34:6).

No, but He should.
Does He ever withhold love from you?

> "For I am sure that neither death nor life, nor angels nor rulers, nor things present nor things to come, nor powers, nor height nor depth, nor anything else in all creation, will be able to

separate us from the love of God in Christ Jesus our Lord." (Romans 8:38-39)

No. That is unbelievable!

The sending of the Son must mean that the Father still loves us despite us. It must mean that the Father's love *for* us is not contingent *upon* us; it originates with Him. God's love is unaffected by the object of His love (us) in the same way that a fountain does not dry up if people stop drinking. We might scamper and skip (or limp or crawl), looking for other water sources, but the Fountain keeps pouring out and inviting sons in for Living Water; eventually we drink.

THE PRODIGAL GOD

prod·i·gal —adjective
1. recklessly extravagant
2. having spent everything

In the parable commonly known as The Prodigal Son, Jesus tells a story of *two* lost sons: (1), the younger brother who took his father's inheritance early, and (2) the elder brother. Both of them, interestingly, separated from the father in their sin—much like my Harper does, and much like we do in our sin against God. The father in the parable represents our Father. The parable shows that we cannot out-sin the Father's grace. As Tim Keller points out, the story "demonstrates the lavish *prodigality* of God's grace. Jesus shows the father pouncing on his son in love not only before he has a chance to clean up his life and evidence a change of heart, but even before he can recite his repentance speech. Nothing, not even abject contrition, merits the favor of God. The Father's love and acceptance are absolutely free." [15]

Let us pursue our children when they sin. Chase them. Run after them. Drown their sin in your love and grace for them. Kiss them. We must still discipline because they need to see their need for the perfect Son. On the other hand, we do not punish them by removing ourselves or our love and affection from them. The Father gave His Son, in your sin, so that you might be in His presence.

> "And [the prodigal son] arose and came to his father. *But while he was still a long way off, his father saw him and felt compassion, and ran and embraced him and kissed him.*" (Luke 15:20)

Irresistible grace.

REFLECTION QUESTIONS

1. How does God's grace stir your affections for him?

2. How have you responded sinfully to your children's sin? Have you repented to God and to them for your sin?

3. How is leading in repentance a measure of God's grace to your children?

4. In pursuing your children, how will you show their need for Jesus? How will you preach the gospel to them?

CHAPTER EIGHT

BE GRACIOUS IN THEIR GROWTH

"I worked harder than any of them . . ."
— *Apostle Paul*

I USED to do hitting lessons for kids. Physically assaulting their dads was a constant temptation. I know your kid hit .675 in tee ball last year, but the third baseman on every team picks his nose, and the first baseman can't catch, and the official scorer does not ever account for errors, and he is five years old! I am sure he will be the next Albert Pujols, but take it down a notch, dad. Close the yearbook and let your kid just play. Your vicarious living is crushing him and annoying me.

I remember sitting in the kitchen, it was late summer, just prior to my senior year of high school. My dad and I were talking about the "Players to Watch For" section of the sports page that had come out that morning on the upcoming high school football season. It was neat to see my name on that list, but my dad's comment to me is something I will never forget. He told me that I didn't have to play football if I didn't want to. "Are you sure you don't want to try something else? Don't think you have to play." It was his way of saying, "I love you regardless of your football abilities, and don't do anything because you falsely think I want you to."

Do you know why Little League Dad exists? It is because he doesn't know his Father. He doesn't know a God that loves him despite his abilities, rather than because of them. Placing a weight (or glory) on his children, Little League Dad unknowingly crushes them—five-year-old t-ball players were never meant to bear the weight of being a god; their abilities or growth can't affirm or define you.

You will be tempted to get your significance from your children's abilities, successes, talents, or intellectual capacity. It will seem loving because you will think, "I just want what's best for you." No, you want what is best for *you*. As a result, you will end up with a five-year-old in a baseball lesson, shame-stricken, as urine runs down his pants from the weight and stress of having to be awesome for his dad (sad, but true story). However, the Gospel shouts that we are *not* awesome for our Dad, and He still loves us.

You can push your children, motivate them, drive them, and even shame them into growing—whether it be growing as an intellectual, an artist, or an athlete, one of two things will happen: 1) They will succeed. They will accomplish what you wanted them to accomplish (straight "A's"; star quarterback; classically trained pianist; the skinny, pretty girl, etc.). Your pushing worked, your motivation succeeded, they are who you wanted them to be—and they will hate you. Even worse, they will end up thinking they need to earn God's love. Or, 2) you will weigh them down so heavily, and run them so hard, that you will crush their spirit, and any "success" they do have will never be enough. Do not distort the image of God by condemning them with the "law" in their growth and maturation.

Your Father is gracious to you in your sanctification and progression as a son. Love is patient (1 Cor. 13:4) because love is God, and God is patient.

He sends His Spirit to "guide [us] into all truth" (John 16:13) because He doesn't expect us to know right now. Though He demands perfection as He is perfect (Matt. 5:48), He makes us His sons by being perfect for us (Heb. 12:2).

The thinking, of course, is that we must push our kids or they will be complacent because sometimes, well, they need a kick-start. However, there is a "kick start" and then there is placing a heavy yoke on the ox and expecting him to run like a stallion—it is a futile effort that will kill the ox. The paradox is that grace motivates us to work harder than any law or burden ever will.

THE APOSTLE PAUL'S GROWTH PROCESS

The earliest letter the Apostle Paul wrote was to the Corinthian church. In it, he calls himself the "least of the apostles" (1 Cor. 15:19). Later, in writing to the Ephesians, he says he is the "least of the saints" (Eph. 3:8). Then, in an even later book (as he aged), he writes to a young pastor, Timothy, that he is the "chief of sinners" (1 Tim. 1:15 KJV). What is going on here? Paul obviously had a lot of growing to do; it was going to take a lot of work in order for him to be successful in the mission God called him to. It would take great effort to grow in godliness, to kill the sin that plagued him. He had "persecuted the church of God" (1 Cor. 15:9). He would have to clock in and not ever clock out, and this he did:

"... I worked harder than any of them ..." (1 Corinthians 15:10)

Why did it seem, then, that he got worse? It seems that his growth was not only stunted, but in reverse. One day he is the "least of the apostles," and the next he is the "chief of sinners." It is one thing to be the worst Apostle, quite another to be the worst human being.

The answer lies in *what he is growing to become.* You see, there is some value in growing in your craft, developing as a leader, cultivating the skills you have been given—proper stewards of all that God has given us is fine and good. However, "while bodily training is of some value, *godliness* is of value in every way, as it holds promise for the present life and also for the life to come" (1 Tim. 4:8). We should encourage and cultivate our children's God-given skills and abilities, but what is far more important is that we, "train [them] for godliness" (1 Tim. 4:7). It was being like his Dad that got the Apostle Paul up in the morning. Being like Dad means seeing the depth of your sin, the height of the cross as its shadow extends and covers over all your sin, and then repenting and believing again in the Gospel. *Repentance is the key to spiritual growth.* Godliness, of course, is not merely bible study and prayer, it is the Christian life informing *all* that we do and it is the same grace of God that saves us that will also develop us as we do what God uniquely knitted us to do.

So, what motivated Paul in all this? What was he driven by? Why was he so committed that he would "endure anything for the sake of the elect" (2 Tim. 2:10); or that he would, like an ox:

" . . . with far greater labors, far more imprisonments, with countless beatings, and often near death. Five times I received at the hands of the Jews the forty lashes less one. Three times I was beaten with rods. Once I was stoned. Three times I was shipwrecked; a night and a day I was adrift at sea; on frequent journeys, in danger from rivers, danger from robbers, danger from my own people, danger from Gentiles, danger in the city, danger in the wilderness, danger at sea, danger from false brothers; in toil and hardship, through many a sleepless night, in hunger and thirst, often without food, in cold and exposure..." (2 Corinthians 11:23-27)

Why would he be willing to go through all that and work harder than anyone else?

Grace.

> "But by the grace of God I am what I am, and *his grace toward me was not in vain. On the contrary, I worked harder than any of them, though it was not I, but the grace of God that is with me.*" (1 Corinthians 15:10)

It was not "pushing him to be the best he could be," nor was it scolding him when not enough people got saved as he preached, that motivated him. Rather, it was grace that compelled Paul to work hard. *He was compelled by grace!*

Image the Father by displaying grace to your children as they grow, grace as they mature, and grace as they develop their gifts and abilities. It is grace upon grace that motivates.

CAL RIPKEN JR. & THE NUMBER 18

We have a VHS tape of a segment the local news station in Oakland did on me and Cal Ripken Jr. I was four years old. The premise of the bit came as the

Baltimore Orioles and Ripken Jr. were in town. At the time, Ripken Jr.'s dad, Cal Sr., was the manager of the Orioles. Obviously, that was pretty neat for Cal Jr. to be playing for his dad.

As they covered the young phenom who would later go on to break a historic record (consecutive games played) in poetic fashion, they played up the father-son angle with me and my dad. Anyway, at the end of the segment (after shots of me and my dad playing catch), I am sitting on my dad's lap in the dugout as my pops interviews me.

"What do you want to be when you grow up?" "A baseball player like you, dad."

"What number do you want to wear?" "Number 24 and 18. Cause I like Rickey Henderson and I like you, dad."

Don't all sons want to do what their dad does? Don't all sons want to be *like* their dad?

"See what kind of love the Father has given to us, *that we should be called children of God; and so we are. Beloved, we are God's children now,* and what we will be has not yet appeared; but we know that when he appears *we shall be like him, because we shall see him as he is.*" (1 John 3:1-2)

REFLECTION QUESTIONS

1. How were you sinfully pushed to grow? Did you end up believing you needed to earn God's love or were you crushed, thinking no type of success would have been enough?

2. How did Jesus perfectly perform on your behalf and extend the love of His Father to you?

3. Do you work hard to earn God's favor or do you work hard because in Christ He has poured out His favor upon you?

4. How does God's grace motivate us to work harder than any law or burden ever will?

CHAPTER NINE

BE GRACIOUS IN DISCIPLINE

"If you use shame on your kids you will train them to hide and deceive. If you use guilt on your kids you will train them to blame others and look away from Jesus to find another atonement. 'Train up your child in the way he should go' . . . they should go to Jesus who removes shame and guilt."
— *Jeff Vanderstelt*

THE LAST time my dad spanked me, the wooden spoon broke, and he deemed the punitive discipline obsolete from then on. How effective could it be if my backside was one-upping the spatula? But for a while it worked.

Having a professional baseball player for a father has its benefits, but his ability to hit things hard with a wooden stick was not one of them. I was a stubborn, hardheaded, first-born child; the noetic effects of Adam's sin were clearly visible in my way of everything being, well, my way. So my dad's abilities to "square up" my bottom with a mini Louisville Slugger were used frequently.

It is interesting, and perhaps a little weird, that I remember being fond of discipline. I was told to go to my room. Sitting on the bed and hearing the kitchen drawer opening at the other end of the house, knowing my fate, was certainly an ominous feeling. However, the experience of discipline itself was not. He would communicate why, he would love me after— not removing his presence or his love from me, but, in fact, drawing nearer. Grace saturated his discipline, as it does with the Father's.

"And have you forgotten the exhortation that addresses you as sons?

'My son, do not regard lightly the discipline of the Lord, nor be weary when reproved by him.

For the Lord disciplines the one he loves, and chastises every son whom he receives.'"

(Hebrews 12:5-6)

Whom does God discipline? He disciplines those He loves. If His kindness leads us to repentance, how much more does His discipline, dripping with grace, benefit his beloved? His grace leads us to worship (for, what is repentance other than the gift of worship?), and His discipline leads us to godliness, which ends in more worship.

How telling is it that God disciplines those He loves? Do not use the language of "punishment" with your children, for Jesus took our punishment. Fathers image their Father by discipline, which is a form of discipleship (same root word). What is discipleship but being formed by grace? Punishment is a penalty to be paid, but discipline is for correction.

However, discipline, at least in the way most of us understand it, is not enough. If all I do is continually, skillfully regulate the behavior of my child, what have I gained? Nothing. Except for maybe a midget Pharisee that blows the whistle on all the "bad" kids.

CHILDREN NEED A PERFECT SON

Parents are agents of God's authority (Eph. 6:1, ". . . in the Lord"; 6:4, ". . . of the Lord"). And the Father is a lawgiver who tells us how we ought to live. There is a rhythm to creation, a way in which He designed it, that if we stay on beat, we will glorify Him and our joy will be full. If we get off beat, things will go bad. The problem is that we have no rhythm, and neither do our children. Nor can we change our children's hearts, because their hearts are dead (Eph. 2:1). They need authority, correction, and loving discipline—but it is not enough! What they really need is a Redeemer. They need a Savior. They need a new heart (Ez. 36:26). A good father, then, is about being a tool in the hands of the Redeemer. Biblical discipline must be showing them their sin and their need for Jesus, so that they might be reconciled to the Father.

WHAT IS SIN?

It is important to first define sin. We don't discipline a child for being a child. Any father (or mother or grandparent for that matter) that chides a child for being childlike is not *for* their children like the Father is *for* the Son or for us, his sons. A little three-year-old girl who is talkative, or a little four-year-old boy that is boisterous is not being sinful—they are just being kids. The Apostle Paul wrote, "When I was a child, I spoke like a child, I thought like a child, I reasoned like a child. When I became a man, I gave up childish ways" (1 Cor. 13:11). Until our children become young men and young women, we shouldn't expect them to "give up childish ways."

Interestingly, the same parent who *will* discipline their four-year-old for an accident *won't* discipline their one-year-old who deliberately disobeys—"She is so young!"

> "Behold, I was brought forth in iniquity,
> and in sin did my mother conceive me."
> (Psalm 51:5)

Your "so young" one-year-old is a sinner in need of a Savior. Our children come out of the womb with broken, bent hearts that default to rebellion, not righteousness. When your little one looks at the electrical outlet and looks back at you after you say "no," and then proceeds to stick her fingers in there anyway, she is wittingly defying your protective authority, and for her joy you must discipline her for that.

We exasperate our children, however, when we discipline them for actions they cannot avoid. Spilling the milk is what young children do, throwing the milk down in rebellion and frustration is what sinners do—there is a distinction. Discerning the distinction is the work of looking past *what happened* and looking *to the heart*.

Our hope and duty as parents is to shepherd our child's heart, not to manage or manipulate their actions. Thus, our discipline should be aimed at the heart and not focused on what they did. This refocusing will, in effect, zoom in our correction towards their rebellious disposition, canceling their childlike ways from our periphery.

How should the discipline look once our shepherd's rod and staff have gotten to the heart? Are there improper uses of the rod and staff? Is our method of discipline an arbitrary decision or do Scripture and the truth of the Gospel inform it?

GOSPEL-INFORMED FUNDAMENTALS

Let us start with the grace of the Father in the Gospel of His Son. By laying a foundation and putting down some Gospel-informed fundamentals, perhaps we can then have a sure footing as we begin the conversation on methods of discipline. We don't want to slip into commonly used justifications like, "My parents did this and I turned out okay," or fall into the way our particular culture views discipline. Jeff Vanderstelt will be helpful in setting this foundation with simplicity and brevity:

> "*Using the consequences of sin to get kids to stop sinning will only lead to more sin. The*

real consequences of sin are guilt, shame, fear of punishment, loss of trust, and broken relationships—your job is not to add more consequences . . ." [16]

"Now the law came in to increase the trespass" (Rom. 5:20). Consequences are not designed to do something for the child; they are designed to do something against them. The Father is for us, He disciplines those He loves.

"Jesus can remove and mend all of these. [Your job] is to lead your children to Jesus who deals with the wages of sin." [17]

We are to "bring them up in the discipline . . . of the Lord" (Eph. 6:4), meaning, we are to lead them to Jesus.

"Fear of punishment as a primary motivator will train your child to seek to avoid pain, suffering, and sacrifice for others. Fear of losing your approval will train your child to live for the approval of others, from worshipping you to worshipping another god." [18]

Grace doesn't punish; grace doesn't remove love. Grace redirects us to the Grace-giver.

"If you use shame on your kids you will train them to hide and deceive. If you use guilt on your kids

you will train them to blame [others] and look away from Jesus to find another atonement. 'Train up your child in the way he should go'—he should go to Jesus who removes shame and guilt." [19]

Grace-saturated, Gospel-informed discipline never leads to what the law leads to, which is guilt, condemnation, shame, despair, and hopelessness. Grace leads to freedom from sin, "For sin will have no dominion over you, since you are not under law but under grace" (Rom. 6:14). The aim of discipline is not behavior modification; it is not having "well-adjusted" kids. Discipline's aim is to the Father and to be *like* the Father: "[God] disciplines us for our good, *that we may share his holiness*" (Heb. 12:10b).

GRACE-LESS DISCIPLINE

Before I describe the biblical way of discipline, let me point out the lack of grace in other forms of discipline. *In general*, these particular methods of discipline tend to lack grace and war against the ways the Father disciplines us. I recognize that godly men and women, even some bible teachers and theologians, would disagree with some of this. With that disclaimer, I would encourage you to run these methods (or their variations) through the grace-grid of God's discipline of His children. Often we are shaped, not by biblical truths, but by cultural influences, and we need to "be transformed by the renewing our minds" (Rom. 12:2).

Time-out: Casting someone from your presence can be a grace (1 Cor. 5:5), but it is a last resort because it is basically an acknowledgment that the unrepentant is not a Christian ("deliver this man to Satan"). Separating your child from the family is the antithesis to what our Father does for us in our sin. Instead, He draws near. He confronts, He disciplines, He corrects, He embraces, and He loves regardless. The message of time out is: If you sin, you are punished by being absent from the family. This does not illustrate the Gospel, which says that if you sin, we will extend grace and forgive you, *welcoming you back in to the family*, since the consequences of your sin already drove you from the family.

Counting: This minimizes sin and teaches our children they can delay obedience. Do you want to teach them to delay obeying God's commands? Sin is serious (start calling your children's sin "sin"). God hates sin. It must be dealt with and not delayed. By delaying obedience, your child delays their own joy: "If you keep my commandments, you will abide in my love, just as I have kept my Father's commandments and abide in his love. These things I have spoken to you, that my joy may be in you, and that your joy may be full" (John 15:10-11).

Bribery/Behavior Modification: Tedd Tripp explains why this is unbiblical: "Since the heart and behavior are so closely linked, *whatever modifies behavior inevitably trains the heart* . . . [With bribery, your child] lives a lust-driven life in which he will perform for ice cream and other goodies."[20] Our children need to be trained to be under God's authority. They need training in *selflessness*, not selfishness—bribery does not train them to look out for the interests of others, only themselves. A promise of reward or a fear of punishment sounds nice, and it works! If you dangle a carrot in front of a donkey or beat it with a stick, you can get it moving down the road. In contrast, the Gospel paints a different picture. Elyse Fitzpatrick wields the brush for us:

> "The Father broke the stick of punishment on His obedient Son's back. Rather than trying to entice us by dangling an unattainable carrot of perfect welcome and forgiveness incessantly in front of our faces, God the Father freely feeds the carrot to us, His enemies. He . . . gives us all the reward and takes upon Himself all the punishment . . . then He tells us, in light of all that He's done, 'Obey.'" [21]

Reactive Responses: Though not a "method," per se, reacting to our children's sin is common. We spank quickly out of anger, we raise our voice, we shame, or we proclaim our disappointment (laying up heavy burdens). Your Father most certainly does not do this. He is patient, long suffering; His impassibility means He never flies off the handle. Reactive responses reveal deep sin in our hearts that make it impossible to lovingly correct our children for their sake; we are reacting for our sake.

GRACIOUS DISCIPLINE

The Gospel is news that is to be heralded, or *proclaimed* — it is good news that needs to be communicated. If our discipline is to be saturated with grace, it *must* have, at its core, a clearly communicated preaching of the Gospel. In addition, because our children do not primarily need more information or more instruction, discipline should be *corrective*. If their hearts were morally neutral, then, perhaps, more information would suffice. However, they are not at a fork in the road deciding which path to take, they already took the wrong path! So they need correction—a redirection—and grace and "kindness that leads to repentance." Finally, both the correction and proclamation are aimed at the *heart* of our children.

> "Do not withhold discipline from a child;
> *if you strike him with a rod, he will not die.*
> If you strike him with the rod,
> you will save his soul from Sheol.
>
> *Hear,* my son, and be wise,
> and *direct your heart in the way* . . .
> . . . *Listen* to your father who gave you life,
> and do not despise your mother when she is old.
>
> My son, *give me your heart,*
> and *let your eyes observe my ways.*"
> (Proverbs 23:13-14, 19, 22, 25)

In just a few verses from a book of the bible written by a father to his son, we see the manifold, gracious discipline of a loving father and the likely[22] response from the son. Any departure from the three-pronged approach walks us into the common error of reductionism—where we emphasize one prong to the neglect of the others. We must correct and proclaim, and do so for the sake of the daily war going on in their hearts.

GRACIOUS CORRECTION

"Folly is bound up in the heart of a child, but the rod of discipline drives it far from him." (Proverbs 22:15)

There is something broken in your child's heart—it is corrupted by sin and it does not know the Father. Communication is not enough. "Folly" interweaves and tangles deep in the heart of your child, enslaving it. Tedd Tripp says,

"Throughout the Proverbs, folly/foolishness is used to describe the person who has no fear of God. The fool is the one who will not hear reproof. The fool is the one who will not submit to authority . . . The fool lacks wisdom (fear of the Lord) . . . The fool's life is run by his desires and fears." [23]

Folly must be *driven* out; it cannot be talked out. Wisdom—or the worship of the Father—must displace it. How? "The rod of correction imparts wisdom . . ." (Prov. 29:15). Wait, I thought the message of the Gospel is that Jesus took the rod for fools like us? Yes, but our children don't know that yet. They need to see that disobedience always leads to pain, but in corrective discipline, the pain will hopefully lead to change:

> "For the moment *all discipline seems painful* rather than pleasant, but later it yields the peaceful fruit of righteousness to those who have been trained by it." (Hebrews 12:11)

The bible takes sin very seriously because God takes sin very seriously. Sin leads to death. This is why Jesus *died* for our sins and wasn't grounded for our sins. Gracious and loving spankings, coupled with communication and the proclamation of the Gospel, goes after their heart. Disciplining in this way redirects our children to Jesus, who took the death they deserved: ". . . if you strike him with a rod, he will not die."

Why? It is because discipline will hopefully lead to their repentance and new life.

How should biblical spanking look? [24]

1. *Take your child to a private place*: Discipline should not rob a child of dignity. You should never discipline in front of the other children in the family. The object is not to humiliate the child.

2. *Tell him specifically what he has done or failed to do*: Spanking should always address a specific attitude or incident.

3. *Secure an acknowledgement from the child of what he has done.* This will take time. My daughter knows she is to obey daddy "first time." I, at the least, want to make sure she can acknowledge that she did not obey daddy.

4. *Remind them why you are spanking:* "Daddy is not mad at you. Daddy loves you. He wants to protect you and he wants this for your joy."

5. *Afterwards, hug and kiss them:* The relationship has been restored. *We cannot be angry with our children, withhold love from them, or "punish" them further by our distance!* That is not grace. You are "correcting" them, not punishing them. You are *for* them, not *against* them.

GRACIOUS PROCLAMATION

> "Hear, my son, and be wise,
> and direct your heart in the way"
> (Proverbs 23:19)

Our children need us to proclaim the truth of the Father's love for them in Christ, which is ultimately their only hope. They need wisdom, yes, but they need Wisdom more. Jesus is the personification of wisdom (Matt. 11:19). He is a wisdom greater than Solomon's

(Matt. 12:42). If our children were to hear about Wisdom and be instructed in wise living, it would "direct [their] heart in the way."

This means that some sort of revelatory communication is necessary. God speaks to us. His words have authority and power, and they accomplish their purpose (Isa. 55:11). God's written (so revealed, communicated) law instructs us (Ps. 32:8). Thus, our discipline must be communicated and not just felt. Do you proclaim the Gospel to your children in the midst of discipline? Do you communicate the truth of the Wise Son who took a fool's punishment? Does "the Word of Christ dwell in you richly, teaching and admonishing one another in all wisdom" (Col. 3:16a)?

When we share the Gospel with our children, we stand both above and beside them: Above them as agents of God's loving authority, and beside them as a fellow sinner in need of grace. The type of communication can vary, as it does in the Scriptures. We see throughout the bible instruction, encouragement, correction, rebuke, entreaty, warning, teaching, and prayer. Most times, our children need a combination of these varying forms of communication in any particular instance.

Seeding our children's hearts with the truth of the grace and mercy of the Gospel will begin to beckon them to the Father as they recognize the Perfect Son. Gracious discipline means that "even in times of correction we'll whisper His name to them through our tears and theirs"[25]—gracious correction always enjoins itself with gracious proclamation.

MY SON, GIVE ME YOUR HEART

"My son, give me your heart,
and let your eyes observe my ways."
(Proverbs 23:25)

Proverbs 4:23 says, "Above all else, guard your heart, for it is the wellspring of life." I would submit to you that it is the parent's duty to guard their children's hearts first, and to show them how. Dad, you cannot bypass your child's heart—you must go directly at it. This is very, very difficult.

"What were you feeling when you hit your sister, Harper?"

Silence. Staring. She's two.

"Were you jealous? Were you frustrated?"

"Elmo!" as she points to the Elmo puppet on the couch.

Getting to her heart is going to take lots of patience, time, foundation laying, and most importantly, her "eyes [observing] my ways." The more you share your heart, the more you walk beside your children as a fellow sinner in need of a Savior, the better chance you will have to get access into their hearts.

"My son, give me your heart," *has* to be the cry of yours! It is *you* that will lead them to the Father. It is *you* that will show them the Son. It is *you* that will labor and toil in prayer that the Spirit would explode in their hearts the truth of the grace of the Gospel, in order that they might know Him and worship Him.

REFLECTION QUESTIONS

1. What is your knee-jerk reaction to discipline or to the truth that God disciplines those who he loves?
2. Have you disciplined your children sinfully in the past? What was your motivation?
3. What aspect of the gospel do you need to believe?
4. How will you discipline your children while modeling the gospel?

CHAPTER TEN

PASTOR DAD

"Truly, I say to you, whoever does not receive the kingdom of God like a child shall not enter it."
— Mark 10:15

AS A toddler my dad would say "Touchdown!" and I would throw both hands up in the air signaling six points, and then he would say "Praise Jesus!" and I would throw both hands up in the air to praise Jesus. That is good parenting. What else does a two-year-old boy need to know?

Two stories stand out in my mind as I think about the legacy my father handed off to me. The first one occurred when I was 22 years old and just a few months away from meeting my future wife. I was about as far away from the Father as I had ever been, and at the same time, so close. One day, Julius Macdougal walked into my office.

I was running an indoor sports arena in the off-season, which was a good job that gave me access to everything I needed in order to train in preparation for the upcoming season. Baby Doc, as Julius was called, walked in. Baby Doc had played for my dad in 1986. I was the batboy for the team at the age of six, so I didn't quite remember him and certainly didn't recognize him so many years later. However, he had seen my name on the door and asked if I was Jim Essian's son.

As we were catching each other up, he told me a story about my father. Apparently in the middle of the season, Baby Doc was in a slump. While on a road trip my dad called Baby Doc up to his hotel room. "I thought I was getting let go," Baby Doc told me. Instead, my dad sat him down on the bed and asked him a random question: Do you pray *with* your wife?

This question stuck with Baby Doc, because he didn't pray with his wife. "I haven't missed a day since, though," he told me. That was 16 years prior to our conversation in my office. Eleven years later I am still telling that story, *and I am* still convicted by it. Even as I write the words now, it is a reminder to pray *with* my wife and not just for her. My dad instructed me later, after I told him about Baby Doc's visit, "Praying with your wife is the most intimate thing you can do with her."

The other story that stands out in regard to my dad's lasting legacy with me happened a few months after Baby Doc's visit. I was in spring training with the Colorado Rockies, still far from God. Sovereignly, the Father put me in community for that month of spring training with some studs that loved Jesus. He used Matt Holiday and Seth Taylor as instruments to graciously pursue me, and he began to draw me back to Himself. I went to a bible study with some of the Rockies players and some guys in the Chicago White Sox camp who also trained in Tucson, Arizona. At the study there was another former player of my dad's, Shawn Boskie.

Boskie told a story about my dad in the study. Boskie wasn't a Christian, in fact, he thought Christian men were effeminate wimps. As a professional athlete—competitive and driven—Christianity wasn't attractive to him at all. However, as he observed my dad throughout the season, he saw a dude, a dude that loved Jesus. Through observing my dad's life *and* doctrine (1 Tim. 4:16), Boskie submitted his life to the Father through the person and work of Jesus.

☙ ❧

Fathers, we must leave a legacy with our children that goes deeper than just church on Sunday mornings and prayer at bedtime. There is a daddy deficit in our world, and only a Gospel renewal will "turn the hearts of fathers to their children" (Mal. 4:6). A truncated Christianity won't do it: Passivity must be stomped out by dads who are sold out for the Father. Impotent men must be empowered by the Spirit of the Father. We need dads to pastor their families, and we need shepherds who follow the Chief Shepherd with great passion and vigilance. This is not negotiable for the church any longer!

PASTOR DAD

It is well-documented that our children, who are raised in the church, are forsaking Her and leaving in droves like a herd seeking spiritual food in a famine. Those who leave seek meaning and purpose in something— anything—that looks meaningful and purposeful. They leave the church because they were starved from true spiritual food and were fed the dessert of endless youth games and "relevant" events, and many never come back. What is happening? The conservative statistics say that 70% will graduate high school and decide church isn't for them.[26] This is a reality and should, at the least, cause parents to question their default choices as to how they relate church, children, and schooling. *You are their primary pastor and teacher*, biblically speaking.

"Hear, O Israel: The LORD our God, the LORD is one. You shall love the LORD your God with all your heart and with all your soul and with all your might. And these words that I command you today shall be on your heart. *You shall teach them diligently to your children*, and shall talk of them when you sit in your house, and when you walk by the way, and when you lie down, and when you rise." (Deuteronomy 6:4-7)

"Hear, my son, *your father's instruction, and forsake not your mother's teaching*, for they are a graceful garland for your head and pendants for your neck." (Proverbs 1:8-9)

"*Train up a child in the way he should go;* even when he is old he will not depart from it." (Proverbs 22:6)

"Fathers, do not provoke your children to anger, but *bring them up in the discipline and instruction of the Lord*." (Ephesians 6:4)

What is explicit and evident in the Scriptures is that parents *are the primary disciplers and teachers* of their children. It is not a pastor, a youth pastor (usually a child himself), or their teachers at school. You are their pastor. Further, the biblical texts reveal to fathers how the Father wants this to look. The bible clearly answers the following questions: "*To what end*" should our parenting and pastoring of our children aim for?, "*In what way*" should we achieve that?, and "*In what context*" should this teaching and pastoring occurs?

PASTOR DAD: TO WHAT END?

"Fathers, do not provoke your children to anger, but bring them up in the discipline and instruction *of the Lord*." (Ephesians 6:4)

First, let us see *to what end* our parenting is aiming and take a closer look at the key that unlocks this verse: ". . . of the Lord."

The Apostle Paul does not mince words here, he doesn't leave us with any options; it is the father's job to pastor and teach his children *in the ways of Jesus*. This would have been an enormously profound statement to his Ephesian readers, as it will be for us.

"The Jews knew what the discipline and instruction of the rabbis looked like. The Greeks knew what the discipline and instruction of the philosophers. But the discipline and instruction *of the Lord? Of Jesus?* What was that?"[27]

Tempting us is not the teaching of the rabbis (the Law) or the Greek philosophers (ethics) per se, but their principles have seeped into our American, Western, and even church cultures. "Be a good girl," is far more ethic-based than grace-based, nor is it *of the Lord*. Math and science, as taught in most schools, has nothing to do with the person and work of Jesus . . .but they do!

The "end" or goal of our parenting is not to raise "good" kids who are valued members of society, or even theologically astute, potentially midget Pharisees. Rather, our hope should be to raise worshipers of Jesus! John Piper said, "Our aim as parents is not merely to stock our kid's heads with knowledge about God, but to inspire our kid's hearts to worship God."[28] How does the good news of the Gospel of Jesus—His person (who He is) and work (what He has done)— inform our parenting? As examples, consider His work in creation, His incarnation, and the power of the Resurrection and its implications:

Creation: The work of Christ in creation is meant to stir us to worship Him (Ps. 19:1). When Jesus spoke the stars and oceans into existence, He wasn't thinking, "I hope this motivates my people to not drink beer and vote Republican." It was meant to provoke our souls to bow at His feet and to raise our hands in great praise!

What if your child's growing understanding in math and science—a knowledge of the laws and glories of the universe— pointed them to just such a response? What foundations might be set if you exclaimed and explained to your joyful three-year old Who it is that created the dogs that they love so much, or Whose idea it was to paint flowers with such diverse and beautiful colors?

Incarnation: How does the condescension of God in Christ, entering into the brokenness and sin of this world contradict and thus, correct, an evolutionary worldview that says the strong should kill off the weak? The incarnation says that the Strong became weak in order to save the weak! The implications of the incarnation lead us to teach our children that we don't join the mockers who bully the weak ("Nice shoes, Johnny! Ha ha ha!"), but we incarnate—enter in—and defend them.

Resurrection: The physical, bodily resurrection of Jesus means that matter matters—the physical world is important. We do justice and mercy, we care for those in need, we serve, sacrifice, and steward because the resurrection is proof that this world matters. We should absolutely instill in our children a hope for Jesus to come back (Rev. 22:20), but not to the extent that we hide out in our Christian bunkers protecting our children from the big, bad world. Because of the resurrection and our calling to be witnesses to it (Acts 1:8), we pray that our children *would have courage and boldness*—not just praying for their protection—but for them to take risks for the cause of Christ.

Of course, the love of the Father demonstrated in the sacrificing of His Son on the cross (Rom. 5:8) both empowers our children and exemplifies to them how to relate with others. The revelation of God in the written Word of God is a great motivation to learn to read. Learning history shows the commonalties of fallen man and the patience of the loving Father with fallen man. Cultivating artistic skills teaches our children to image their creative Father, and on and on we could go. We pastor and parent our children in a way that leads them to a big, glorious Father to worship through the person and work of the Son, and by the power of the Holy Spirit.

PASTOR DAD: IN WHAT WAY?

"Fathers, do not provoke your children to anger, but *bring them up in the discipline and instruction* of the Lord." (Ephesians 6:4)

The goal of our parenting is to show our children their need for a Savior and for them to worship that Savior. The way to achieve that is through *discipline* and *instruction.* The word for discipline, *paideia,* means to "nurture" or "train." The word for instruction, *nouthesia,* means to "correct" or "warn."

Let us look at *paideia,* or nurturing and training first. It may seem odd for fathers to consider themselves "nurturing" to their children, that is mom's job, isn't it? Yes, of course, but it is yours also. In fact, the Apostle Paul—a great pastor and dudely dude (see 2 Cor. 11:23-28)—was nurturing to his people:

> "But we were gentle among you, *like a nursing mother taking care of her own children.* So, being affectionately desirous of you, we were ready to share with you not only the gospel of God but also our own selves, because you had become very dear to us." (1 Thessalonians 2:7-8)

Nurturing our children, then, would look much like what we spoke of in the section on being gentle. However, it also means that we are *affectionate.* Fathers, please hear this! You cannot over-hug or over-kiss your children! If your father's lack of affection (or improper affection) has distorted and skewed your affections towards your children, then please wash in the waters of the Father's affection for you! God sings over you (Zep. 3:17), and Jesus wanted to embrace His people,

"How often would I have gathered your children together as a hen gathers her brood under her wings . . ." (Matt. 23:37). Kiss your sons and daughters, embrace and hug them. My little Harper daily requests, "Daddy rock Harper," and I do!

Nurturing our children also means we "share with you not only the gospel of God but also *our own selves.*" Paul is connecting the teaching of the Gospel with the way our lives teach others. He connects the two again in his admonition to a young pastor, Timothy:

> "Keep a close watch on yourself and on the teaching. Persist in this, for by so doing you will save both yourself and your hearers." (1 Timothy 4:16)

We nurture our children by our lives matching up with our doctrine. "Do what I say, not what I do," is damning to ourselves and to our children. Have you repented to your children yet and asked them to forgive you? Have you not sinned against them? I was repenting to my daughter before she could walk—that is not evidence of how great a parent I am, but how bad! Do they ever see you read your bible? As Mark Driscoll says,

"A wise dad may realize that a personal quiet time for himself is unwise; rather than hiding away in a quiet place to read the bible, it is often best to do so in the noisy living room where the kids can see and climb on their dad while he reads the bible . . . his children will be more likely to ask him questions about God and life because they see that he possesses answers from God's Word."[29]

In addition to nurturing our children, to *paideia* them, we must train them. This is the same word used in Hebrews chapter 12 in regards to discipline, so I would point you back to the previous chapter. As well, we train our children with the Word of God:

> "All Scripture is breathed out by God and profitable for teaching, for reproof, for correction, and for training (*paideia*) in righteousness, that the man of God may be complete, equipped for every good work." (2 Timothy 3:16-17)

We are called to teach and explain the Scriptures to our children in order to train them in righteousness, that they might be "equipped for every good work." Deuteronomy 6:6-7 is explicit, "And these words that I command you today shall be on your heart. You shall teach them diligently to your children . . ."

What do family devotionals look like for you? Do you have the Jesus Storybook Bible yet? Have you begun to teach the truths of the Scriptures so that when your children can begin to understand more, and perhaps sit through a short family worship time, they aren't being introduced to completely foreign concepts and stories?

All Scripture is about, and points to, Jesus (John 5:39). Do you talk about Jesus? Do they speak of Him at all? Do they know you gather with the church to worship His name? Some of you may say, "But they are so young, they can't understand it." What about difficult doctrines such as the Trinity? Russell Moore explains why we shouldn't shy away from teaching our children seemingly difficult theology:

> "Children are open to mystery and paradox in ways adults often aren't. Children explore the world around them with a wide-eyed sense of wonder. They don't comprehend it all, and they know they don't comprehend it all . . . with that the case, we ought to boldly say to our children, "God is One and God is three. I can't fully explain all of that because that's how big and mysterious God and his ways are. Isn't that wonderful?" When your child says,

"That boggles my mind," don't respond with a worried handwringing but with a twinkle in your eye. "I know!" you say. "Me too! Isn't that wild, and great!"[30]

Therefore, to *paideia* our children, to train them, the Scriptures must be opened, the truths exposited, and the Gospel proclaimed. You are to pastor your children, dad.

As well, fathers are to bring their children up in the *nouthesia* of the Lord, that is, to warn and correct them. Again, the Apostle Paul speaks of this as a pastor to his people: "I do not write these things to make you ashamed, but to admonish (*noutheteo*) you as my beloved children" (1 Cor. 4:14).

Though *nouthesia* in Ephesians 6 is translated as "*instruction*," it means much more than "teaching." It means to counsel our children in a way that leads them to repentance in order to change a course they are on, and revert their course to the proper end goal, which is worshiping the Father!

"[It is Christ] we proclaim, warning (*noutheteo*) everyone and teaching everyone with all wisdom, that we may present everyone mature in Christ" (Colossians 1:28)"

Notice that warning (*noutheteo*) and teaching are seen alongside each other. It is a lazy daddy that only warns his children and doesn't teach them also. If you are constantly saying, "no!" but never teaching them how to do something, or how to obey, then you take the easy road, and you rob your children of their primary teacher—you!

Also, notice that the end goal is to "present [them] mature in Christ", because our instruction is "of the Lord." If our aim is for our children to be worshipers of the Father, then we *must* correct and warn them—it is not an option. Dads, you cannot be the "good cop" and let your wife be the "bad cop." This is, primarily, your duty. However, correcting and warning is always dripping with grace and mercy; it is always the loving redirection of a gentle daddy. In fact, as John Piper points out[31], we should sing it:

"Let the word of Christ dwell in you richly, teaching and admonishing (*noutheteo*) one another in all wisdom, *singing psalms and hymns and spiritual songs*, with thankfulness in your hearts to God." (Colossians 3:16)

Dad, lavish your children with affection—share your life, not just your doctrine—sing truths, corrections, and warnings to your little one that they might worship their Heavenly Daddy! What a great joy it is to lead our children to the Father!

PASTOR DAD: IN WHAT CONTEXT?

"Hear, O Israel: The LORD our God, the LORD is one. You shall love the LORD your God with all your heart and with all your soul and with all your might. And these words that I command you today shall be on your heart. You shall teach them diligently to your children, *and shall talk of them when you sit in your house, and when you walk by the way, and when you lie down, and when you rise.*" (Deuteronomy 6:4-7)

Pastor Dad, there is not a time that you relinquish that title. These three verses are the framework for discipleship, and God specifically includes the discipling of children. First, we are to love the One, True God with all of our being. The rest of the bible teaches us how. Second, *we* are to teach others. Who is the "*we*"? Anyone that would have heard or read God's command. But specifically parents!

"You shall teach them *diligently* to your children . . ."

Are you diligent in teaching your children how to love God? Do you tell them, over and over, that He loved them first? Do you know how to teach them *diligently*? You do this by teaching them *all the time in every place.*

When you sit in your house. For example, at the dinner table you don't let your four-year old just answer, "fine" to every question. You keep pursuing their heart, you find ways to point them to Jesus, and you remind them of God's love for them. While watching television or a movie, you are looking for shepherding moments; you can pause the movie to talk about what just happened.

When you walk by the way. Wherever you go there will be moments, opportunities, and circumstances to instruct your children—don't waste them! Why don't we push little Daniel at the park? Why do you need to obey daddy the first time? Do you see that daddy on his phone over there not playing with his daughter, how does that make you feel? When we go to City Group we want you to have fun, but we also want you to play quietly so mommy and daddy can talk about Jesus.

When you lie down and when you rise. What a joy to bookend the days for our children with reminders of the love of the Father! When I put Harper to bed I read to her, often from the Jesus Storybook Bible, and I pray for her. She asks me to, "Play with Harper's hair," and we talk about the day.

What is obvious from Deuteronomy 6:4-7 is that pastoring our children never stops. They hear our instruction, and they observe our lives. By proxy, we are saying, "Follow me, as I follow Christ," (1 Cor. 11:1). *We cannot outsource the pastoring of our children.* Aside from God's commands throughout the Scriptures for the parents to be the teachers and disciplers of their children, it is logically foolish. As one pastor points out,

"Generally, churches with Sunday-focused kids ministries spend 50-100 hours per year (of the 8,760 hours in the year) with kids . . . But what happens in the rest of a child's week when the teacher isn't there? Who hears about getting made fun of on the playground? Who's there to encourage the student in the midst of a specific high school struggle? At minimum, if a child is in school until 4pm and goes to bed at 8pm, parents interact with their kids 1460 hours a year! Parents see the daily struggles. Parents have conversations in the car. Parents are asked the hard questions. Parents deal with the specifics, the scenarios, the struggles, the sins. Parents meet their child—every single day —where the real-life rubber hits the road."[32]

It is a great responsibility to pastor our children, but God's instruction to parents is not solely for the children. Even in our parenting, as we teach, our children teach us. Our Father is so gracious He pastors us as we pastor our children. There are some things only a child can teach us:

> "At that time Jesus declared, "I thank you, Father, Lord of heaven and earth, that you have hidden these things from the wise and understanding and revealed them to little children . . ." (Matthew 11:25)

> "And calling to him a child, he put him in the midst of them and said, "Truly, I say to you, unless you turn and become like children, you will never enter the kingdom of heaven. Whoever humbles himself like this child is the greatest in the kingdom of heaven . . ." (Matthew 18:2-4)

Pastor your children, and as you do, receive the loving shepherding of your Father. There is grace upon grace that overflows with more grace—you are a child too, dad: "Truly, I say to you, whoever does not receive the kingdom of God like a child shall not enter it" (Mark 10:15).

REFLECTION QUESTIONS

1. Have you viewed yourself as the primary discipler and teacher of your home? What hinders you from leading in this way? Is it comfort, approval, security, or power?

2. If you are going to pastor your family in this way what do you need to repent of and what will that repentance look like specifically?

3. As the Father seeks those to worship him in spirit and truth how does this change how you view the aim of your parenting? What has been your guiding principles for parenting up to this point (to be "good" kids, successful, socially normal, perform well where you didn't, etc.)?

4. In light of all this what aspect of the gospel do you need to believe now (who God is, what he has done in Jesus on your behalf, who he has made you)?

5. What will you determine now for nurturing and training to look like (expressed affection, "daddy-dates", prayers, repentance, bible reading, devotionals, etc.)?

6. How will you warn, teach, and shepherd your child's heart toward worshipping Jesus?

CONCLUSION

"The good news is not that God is our model of fatherhood, but that in Christ he has become the Father even of bad Christian dads."
— *Michael Horton*

"BE PERFECT as your Heavenly Father is perfect" (Matt. 5:48). But we can't! Perhaps at this point your heart is both soaring with the colliding truth of the Father's love for you and sinking with the demand to "image" His love to our children.

Do not heed the condemnation. Do not believe the lie. Do not sink into darkness that you are blind to the gospel truths I hoped to saturate these pages with. Our Father does not love you in these ways because of your perfection. He has chosen to love you—before galaxies were declared into existence, before the foundations of the earth (Eph. 1:4). Only Jesus was the perfect Son. He is the image of the invisible God (Col. 1:15) and the exact imprint of His nature (Heb. 1:3). The Father and the Son glorified each other from eternity past and will do so to eternity future.

We are *redeemed* images of God—made glorious, yes, not because of our perfection but for our union with the Perfector (Heb. 12:2). We ride on the coattails of Big Brother, He is the "firstborn among many brothers" and we are "heirs with Christ," adopted as sons, receiving all the benefits of a son because of Christ.

The grace of the Father both saves us from our distorted images of Him to our children, and it empowers and compels us to rightly image Him for our children's sake and ours— and, ultimately, for His Glory.

"Unless the Lord builds the house,
Those who build it labor in vain.
Unless the Lord watches over the city,
The watchman stays awake in vain.
It is in vain that you rise up early
And go late to rest,
Eating the bread of anxious toil;
For he gives to his beloved sleep.

Behold, children are a heritage from the Lord,
The fruit of the womb a reward.
Like arrows in the hand of a warrior
Are the children of one's youth.
Blessed is the man
Who fills his quiver with them!"
(Psalms 127)

God the Father is a model for all fatherhood. However, it *cannot* be just that! It is the Lord that will build your house—otherwise you will build in vain. It is the Lord that watches over your city. Your wife, your children, their spiritual sustenance, their maturation, their salvation, all of it is the oversight of the Lord, the Good Shepherd.

"...if God's fatherhood is only a model for us, it cannot come as good news but only as further condemnation of our own poor performance. The good news is that this God, the Father of Jesus, is now our Father because of his love and the obedience rendered by his Son. In Christ, we do not dread this Father's displeasure as condemnation and judgment, but feel his fatherly hand in redemption and correction. In other words, *the good news is not that God is our model of fatherhood, but that in Christ he has become the Father even of bad Christian dads.*"[33]

Oh what great news! God is your Father! It is not because you apply the truths of this book perfectly, or because your children are the "well-behaved" kids, the smart ones, or the godly ones. Rather, because you are in Christ, you are in the Perfect Son, and now have the Perfect Father.

Furthermore, like a young son hammering his first nail, his father's hand wrapped around his—the father's dexterity and strength doing all the work—yet the son takes joy in accomplishing this great first feat of manhood, of sinking the nail deep into the wood with a smile on his face or a look of determination, completely empowered by his dad. In the same way, we are empowered by the Father to father our children who are our image-bearers. It is in our weakness that He is strong, and the nail cuts through the hard wood of their hard hearts. It is the edification of something great, and something that will bring glory to the Heavenly Father and great joy to you, the earthly father.

Leave this legacy with your family, impart it, pray it in, sweat and toil for it, "do not grow weary in doing good" (Gal. 6:9).

Jonathan Edwards was, perhaps, the greatest thinker and theologian in American history. He was a catalyst for the First Great Awakening, a revival that hit New England in the late 1700s, but he was first a husband and a daddy. He died young (at least from our finite perspective), at the age of 55. On his deathbed he called his daughter Lucy to him and said,

> "Dear Lucy, it seems to me to be the will of God that I must shortly leave you; therefore give my kindest love to my dear wife, and tell her, that the uncommon union, which has so long subsisted between us, has been of such a nature as I trust is spiritual and therefore will continue forever: and I hope she will be supported under so great a trial, and submit cheerfully to the will of God. *And as to my children, you are now to be left fatherless, which I hope will be an inducement to you all to seek a Father who will never fail you.*"

His wife Sarah, was herself quite ill when she received the news by letter of her husband's death. She wrote to her daughter Esther in response:

> "What shall I say: A holy and good God has covered us with a dark cloud. O that we may kiss the rod, and lay our hands on our mouths! The

Lord has done it. He has made me adore his goodness that we had him so long. But my God lives; and he has my heart. *O what a legacy my husband, and your father, has left to us! We are all given to God: and there I am and love to be.* Your ever affectionate mother, Sarah Edwards."

Would that this be our legacy as fathers as well. That our job would be done as our wife and children are "all given to God." That as failing fathers we would, through both life and doctrine, lead them to a Father "who will never fail you." Is this not the train we are on? Is this not the direction we are to go?

With lenses off, sin removed by the blood of the Son, and clarity to see the True Father, relish in His generosity, His gentleness, and His grace to you; and by the power of the Holy Spirit, image the Father to your children. Grace be with you.

REFLECTION QUESTIONS

1. What is God saying to you?
2. What are you going to do about it?
3. Who are you going to share it with?

ENDNOTES

1. *http://www.desiringgod.org/blog/posts/learning-fatherhood-from-the-father-of-fatherhood*

2. Father Hunger, Douglas Wilson, (191)

3. Wilson, Douglas (2012-05-01). Father Hunger: Why God Calls Men to Love and Lead Their Families (Kindle Locations 2273-2279).

4. C.S Lewis, *The Weight of Glory*

5. What is "Success" in Parenting Teens? *http://www.ccef.org/what-success-parenting-teens*

6. *Eyes Wide Open, p63-64, Steve Dewitt*

7. *He knows!*
   a. Matthew 26:47-56, 69-75.
   b. Luke 22:39-46.
   c. Matthew 8:20.
   d. John 7:3-5.
   e. 1 Peter 3:18, Acts 17:2-3, John 19:17-30.
   f. John 4:8.
   g. Matthew 4:1-11.
   h. John 1:10-11, 2:18-22, 13:6-9.

8. *http://theresurgence.com/2011/11/13/the-bible-is-shockingly-honest-and-gloriously-hopeful*

9. *http://marshill.bandcamp.com/track/in-tenderness*

10. What is "Success" in Parenting Teens?
    http://www.ccef.org/what-success-parenting-teens

11. What is "Success" in Parenting Teens?
    http://www.ccef.org/what-success-parenting-teens

12. *Paul Tripp, Parenting: It's Never and Interruption*

13. *https://vimeo.com/43635793*

14. *https://vimeo.com/43635793*

15. *The Prodigal God, Tim Keller, (28)*

16. *http://www.joshcousineau.com/jeff-vanderstelt-on-parenting-via-twitter/*

17. *ibid*

18. *ibid*

19. *ibid*

20. *Shepherding a Child's Heart, Tedd Tripp, (60-61)*

21. *Give Them Grace, Elyse Fitzpatrick & Jessica Thompson, (108)*

22. *The Proverbs are full of "truisms." They are not all, necessarily, promises. For example, "Train up a child in the way he should go; even when he is old he will not depart from it" (Prov. 22:6) is not a promise*

that our children will never leave the faith (or even enter it!) if we train them perfectly or even properly. However, it is a truism. It is a practical truth to obviously adhere to.

23. *Shepherding a Child's Heart, Tedd Tripp, (102)*

24. *This list is adapted from Shepherding a Child's Heart, Tedd Tripp, (147-148)*

25. *Give Them Grace, Elyse Fitzpatrick & Jessica Thompson, (99)*

26. *See http://www.schoolandstate.org/SBC/Pinckney-WeAreLosingOurChildren.htm & http://www. lifeway.com/ArticleView?storeId=10054&catalog Id=10001&langId=-1&article=LifeWay-Research-finds-reasons-18-to-22-year-olds-drop-out-of-church among others*

27. Give Them Grace, Elyse Fitzpatrick & Jessica Thompson, (84)

28. *http://www.desiringgod.org/resource-library/conference-messages/parenting-for-the-glory-of-god-part-1*

29. *Pastor Dad, Mark Driscoll (28)*

30. *http://www.russellmoore.com/2012/09/10/how-do-you-explain-the-trinity-to-children/*

31. *http://www.desiringgod.org/resource-library/taste-see-articles/more-thoughts-for-fathers-on-ephesians-64*

32. *http://www.gospelcentereddiscipleship.com/kids-in-the-family-of-god-part-two/*

33. *Michael S. Horton, Good News for Bad Dads*

ACKNOWLEDGEMENTS

I AM just a dumb jock so I needed a lot of help with this book. Thank you Caitlyn O'Loughlin for your many (free) hours editing the first few drafts. Thank you Stephany Chastine for editing the last one.

Thank you Jessica McCorkle, Daniel Reynolds, and Matt Allen for your researching and finding quotes.

Thank you Ryan Keeney for your work on the reflection questions.

Thank you to Nick Ostermann for checking the manuscript for theological accuracy. Your friendship, encouragement, and partnership in the Gospel in Fort Worth is comforting.

My sweet wife, Heather, continually encouraged me during the writing process and is a constant wise voice, tender heart, and listening ear—she is a strong helper.

Paradox family, I love you and truly believe you are the easiest church to pastor.

Harper and Hollis, I don't love you this much, no, not this much . . . but THIS MUCH!

And, finally, I love you mom and dad.

ABOUT THE AUTHOR

JIM ESSIAN planted The Paradox Church in 2011 and serves as Lead Pastor. The Paradox is an Acts 29 Network church in Downtown Fort Worth, TX. Jim played eight years of professional baseball in the Kansas City Royals, Los Angeles Dodgers, and Detroit Tigers organizations, prior to planting a church. Jim and his wife, Heather, have two girls, Harper and Hollis.

Was Your Father Generous, Gentle, and Gracious?

Your Heavenly Father is. The problem is that we see the Father through our earthly father. We are all given lenses at some point in our childhood, and we still wear them even as we begin to parent our own children. The lenses gray our understanding of the Father. Who is He? What does He think of me? Does He accept me? Is He proud of me? What does He want from me?

Herein lies the beauty of the gospel: In Christ, our lenses are removed so we can clearly see the Father, and, in Christ, the Father puts on lenses and sees us through His perfect Son!

This means that in the Gospel we can see what the Father is like. God the Father not only exemplifies fatherhood, but He empowers us in the Gospel to father like Him. If we can see the Father, we can image the father to our children.

So what is the Father like? Let's remove the lenses and see.

CPSIA information can be obtained at www.ICGtesting.com
Printed in the USA
BVOW08s2244231013

334461BV00002B/8/P

9 781935 909453